MAXWELL'S HISTORY OF THE WORLD IN 366 LESSONS

MAXWELL'S HISTORY OF THE WORLD IN 366 LESSONS

(AN EDITED VERSION OF THE MAXWELL'S DAY BLOG 2012)

PETER MAXWELL
M. J. TROW

EST. 2019

BLKDOG

www.blkdogpublishing.com

ABOUT THE AUTHOR:

Peter Maxwell is currently Head of Sixth Form at Leighford High School, Leighford, West Sussex. He has been in post for all of this century and most of the last and studied under Socrates (See 5 February on how to calculate his age). Having obtained a stonkingly good degree in History from the University of Cambridge, he got his first teaching job at Dotheboys Hall, Yorkshire.

He was moved to blog for the year 2012 because most of the girls of Ten Pea Zed started worrying even before the Christmas Holidays 2011 had begun that the world would end on 20/12 2012. There is no need to say, at this point, that it didn't, but the fact that Mad Max thought it worth starting a blog stopped the girls from heading off in a body to a mountain in Peru and actually, dinosaur though he is where all things digital are concerned, he quite got to like it, in the end. Which it wasn't, as previously announced.

He is married with one son and a cat and he lists his hobbies as some soldiers and minding your own business. The rest is History.

In this slightly updated version, Maxwell has acquired a second cat, Bismarck, who has unaccountably not been eaten by the mighty Metternich.

Also of note, to say it again and one more time and for clarification – this was first written in 2012. So please, when doing the maths, don't think 'Aha!' and fire off angry reviews. It isn't a mistake, it's just the good old passage of time.

ABOUT THE EDITOR:

M.J. Trow used to bill himself as the only Welshman who can't play rugby or sing. Since then, he has met a lot more who can't either. Born in the Rhondda Valley, he moved around muchly as a child and obtained a stonkingly good degree in History from King's College, London. He got his first teaching job at Stanborough School, Welwyn Garden City and hung up his chalk years ago when he realised that there was to be a financial crisis and his razor-sharp business mind was needed in Wall Street.

He is the author of over one hundred books, all History related, veering from crime fiction to true crime via biography. He lives in the Isle of Wight with his better half and his wife, Carol, aka the equally successful writer and editor, Maryanne Coleman. Until recently, the couple lectured regularly on cruise ships. Then, they stopped cruise ships.

He has been a personal friend of Mad Max Maxwell for years and all they disagree on historically is the role of Hegelian dialectic in the defenestration of Prague.

So, that's all right.

JANUARY

Peter Maxwell & M. J. Trow

Jan 1

For those who are privy to the strange world of Peter Maxwell, let me just explain that I don't know how this works, how my daily jottings will get out there into what people apparently call cyberspace. I just know that Mrs B has told me what keys to press and occasionally I find that there is somewhere for me to write. Today is one of the lucky days. I'm sure that on others I will inadvertently end up buying a used Fiesta on eBay, but since I am here, I will do what I intend to do each day (with a following wind and a bit of help from passing IT staff, wives and my increasingly computer literate child and, rather more worryingly, cat) and that is to share a few thoughts on historical events from the Day in Question. So, on this day ...

Paul Revere was born, 277 years ago. If you're British, you've probably never heard of him; if you're American, he's right up there with Babe Ruth and Mother Teresa. He was a silversmith and Ratfink who gave the game away in the War of American Independence by galloping all over the villages of New England, shouting, 'The British are coming! The British are coming!' The more sensible Americans who heard him just adhered to the later World War Two advice – 'Keep Calm and Carry On Drinking Coffee.'

> **Incidentally, as they pointed out in the (at first) excellent series *Sleepy Hollow* on Amazon Prime, which first aired in 2014, Revere did *not* say that because, technically, *all* colonists were still British then. He actually said 'The redcoats are coming!' Doesn't mean he wasn't a traitor, however!**

In other news ... in 1961 those mysterious fellows who design and mint coins had one less job to do. They stopped making farthings, the smallest and dinkiest coin, which, the Oldies will remember, had a cute little Jenny Wren on it (and of course Her Majesty, God Bless Her, on the other side). Depending on your take life, this was either a sensible move because you hadn't been able to buy anything for a farthing for at least a century or it was part of the international conspiracy that was to lead to decimalization, the advent of the European Union and the End of Civilization.

Well ... that was surprisingly simple. The next surprise will be when I am here again tomorrow, with some January 2 facts. Perhaps I ought to just stay in front of this screen all night, to be sure.

And finally, don't forget; if you can read this, thank a teacher.

Jan 2

I'm going to try not to be amazed each day that the blog goes on – bets have been placed amongst colleagues and the family that I will have forgotten how to do it by the end of January. Well, keep watching this space, because I intend to do the whole year. At least.

So, what was happening on this day in history?

Tex Ritter died on this day in 1974. White hats were doffed all over the Western world at his passing because he represented the kind of guy we all wanted to be – a singing cowboy. Picture the scene: the Indians are on the warpath; outlaws are rustling cattle and holding up the Overland Stage; Sleazeball Joe Macready is buying up all the property on Main Street – but none of this matters, because Tex is bursting into song and his little Dogies are getting along just fine. They don't make westerns like his any more – in fact, they hardly make Westerns, with the very creditable exception last year of *True Grit* and that was a remake – and we're all the sorrier for it.

> *Spoof* Westerns, now – that's different. Check out (as cowboys never used to say) *A Million Ways to Die in the West* (2014) and you'll laugh all the way to Tombstone.

In other news ... Cardinal Richelieu (he's the baddie in the red outfit in the Musketeers films) set up the Academie Francaise in 1635 to safeguard the purity of the French language. Which is why, on the other side of the Channel, they have '*le weekend*' during which they watch '*le football*' whilst eating '*le fast food*'. So that was a job well done – let's hear it for the Cardinal!

See you tomorrow!

Jan 3

It was a busy day in the past, was 3rd January. Martin Luther (who was absolutely no relation to the black Civil Rights leader of nearly the same name, as I keep telling Ten Bee Four) really blew it 591 years ago today when the Pope finally lost patience and excommunicated him. In a long story cut short, Luther was a Dominican monk, a guy on the inside who knew exactly how corrupt the Catholic church was. Today, he would set up his blog and his twitter and get himself on Andrew Marr's Sunday TV chat show and tell us all about it. Then, he nailed his 95 theses (bullet points) to the door of Wittenburg cathedral because anybody who was anybody passed that way.

Astonishingly, having implied the Catholic church was a waste of time and that priests were pointless, he got off Scot (or rather, German) free and spent the rest of his life throwing inkpots at the Devil and suffering appallingly from constipation.

Some historians now claim that the 95 Theses story is a myth. Who are these namby-pamby killjoys who don't recognise a bit of Fake News when they read it?

And serve him right.

In other news ... Marcus Tullius Cicero was born in 106 BC. I used to think he was ancient Rome's greatest orator. Then I read a book on Cleopatra and found that he whinged about her because she forgot to lend him a book. Bearing in mind she had the biggest library in the world (at Alexandria) and was kept kind of busy ruling a vast empire and keeping the avaricious, thuggish Romans at bay, it's hardly surprising that she overlooked the loan of a book. Cicero didn't see it that way and said nasty things about her in letters to friends. Eventually, somebody cut his head off and sent it as a present to Marc Antony's wife (not Cleopatra – the other one). Who wouldn't be delighted to receive a present like that: she stuck a hat pin in the dead orator's tongue, making her point.

Jan 4

Back to school – another day, another dollar. Wednesdays aren't too bad as I have no contact whatsoever with the class from hell, Nine Zed Are, so this is as good a start as can be wished. So, in other times, what happened on this day?

I've always found it rather odd that Isaac Newton, who was born on this day 369 years ago, should be regarded as one of the most brilliant minds in history. All right, he was passably competent at mathematics and gravitational apples, but his chemistry was far below that of the average Year 7 kid. He believed in elixirs of life, alchemists' stones and long-leggity beasties. His *Principia Mathematica* has been hailed as one of the Most Important Books of All Time – which is equally odd because it was written in Latin and only about six people in Britain at the time could read it.

Today, nobody can.

P.S, (That's Post Scriptum to you) this was also the day another great scientist, Galileo Galilei, died. But curiously, he and Newton never met. I always think that Mr and Mrs Galilei thought their little boy was so good, they nearly named him twice. Why didn't they choose another name like Rainbow, Moon Unit, Zabaglione? Incidentally, he was born in the same year as Shakespeare and Marlowe, but he never met them either.

In other news ... Jakob Grimm, one of the famous Brothers, was born in 1785. The importance of these guys is that their collection of folk tales told it like it was – a nasty world of rape, murder and terrifying demons. This is what kids want to read about – not the schmaltzy stuff of Mother Goose and Walt Disney.

Jan 5

That's it – enough! One day back and the Christmas spirit is well and truly gone. According to the statisticians (who, let's face it, aren't real people at all) the worst day of the entire year is coming up next week. Apparently, this is because all of the Christmas bills arrive on the mat and the nation falls into a depression. Well, I just want to say the worst day was the first day of school, which was yesterday. So the thought of another, worse day coming up next week is not really a nice thought at all. So, let's have a little think about this day in history, rather than this day today!

One of the great lines in History coming up. The 30th President of the United States, John Calvin Coolidge, died today in 1933. Dorothy Parker asked, 'How could they tell?' They don't ask them like that any more!

In other news ... England played Australia in the world's first one day cricket match in 1871. They were actually trying to do us all a favour by speeding up a sport that is the least watchable of all (after golf and motor racing). Now, if they would just introduce the concept of tip and run, it *could* be really exciting – and, better still, all over in half an hour! And darts, I should have said. And snooker. Shot put. Cycling speed trials .... the list goes on, but cricket is pretty near the top, however you cut it. Olympics this year. Goody, goody!

Jan 6

Twelfth Night and about time too. At last we can take down the Christmas Tree, now needleless and looking like a nuclear blast survivor and stash the tinsel away for another year. Nolan and the Count (son and cat, in that order for those of you unfamiliar with the Maxwell ménage) are already counting the weeks until next Christmas but let them count; as long as I don't run another pine needle into my foot for around another forty nine weeks, that is enough for me. The sole point of this day is that it gave

Will Shaxper of Stratford a title for one of his hilariously funny comedies. How we laughed.

In other news ... Sigmund Freud, dream analyst and inventor of the slip, grandfather of the late Lucien and Clement, wrote in 1938, 'What progress we are making. In the Middle Ages they would have burned me. Now they are content with burning my books.'

'They' of course were the Nazis who had just taken over Freud's native Austria in the *Anschluss* (Union). He was wrong of course – within five years the Nazis would be burning people as well.

Incidentally, they'd all got Freud's number. He was in the Black Book, a list of undesirables living in Britain drawn up by the SS in 1940. Had Operation Sealion worked and Hitler actually invaded Britain, Freud would have got his after all. Actually, though, he wouldn't. Although the compilers of the Black Book seemed unaware, he died in his bed in September 1939.

Jan 7

I have just run another pine needle into my foot – my word, that year went by quickly. But wait, it isn't next Christmas yet, it is merely an inadequately hoovered carpet, courtesy of Mrs B, that has caused me to resort yet again to the tweezers. Perhaps I should keep quiet about her domestic shortcomings, as it is she who keeps me up and running, IT-wise. You can't have everything. Just because she is a whizz with computers, that is no reason to suppose she can wield a Henry with any skill.

So, to History. In 1558 on this day, the British lost their last foothold in France – the town of Calais. The Queen, Mary Tudor (not called 'Bloody' for another three centuries, by the way) was heartbroken. Everybody else was delighted. As we still are.

In other news ... George Washington was unanimously elected the first president of the newly formed United States 223 years ago today. It was unfortunate that his name was George, or he might have considered accepting the crown the colonists offered him. It would have been a bit naff, not to say confusing, to set up another King George having spent time, money and blood to get rid of the old one.

Ironically, of course, the American Presidents of Washington's future were to have more power than any king of England ever had.

And finally ... in 1990 the Leaning Tower of Pisa was closed as the rate of lean was increasing to the point where it could easily have become the Horizontal Tower of Pisa. As a tourist attraction, it wouldn't have had quite the same pull, somehow.

Jan 8

212 years ago today, the first soup kitchens were opened for the London poor. Isn't it nice to think that dear old George III's government was so kind to teachers?

In other news ... Now, I don't mind too much that the Americans beat us at the battle of New Orleans today in 1812. I think they got lucky and they used sneaky tactics like hiding behind cotton bales, trees and so on and they had Charlton Heston to lead them (or is that just in the film *The Buccaneer?*).

No, what really annoyed me was Lonnie Donegan who had a hit with *The Battle of New Orleans* in the 1950s. Donegan was an Englishman born in Essex and it would have been nice if he'd recorded something from the English point of view. Just to let my American reader know that you aren't the only one to have had a Benedict Arnold in your midst.

Today being Sunday, we will be enjoying our usual Sunday game of Scrabble, at which I will be trounced by Mrs Troubridge, come round specially from next door for the fun. She may be a million years old and as mad as a box of frogs, but my word that woman can play Scrabble! She knows more eight letter words containing an ex, a zed, a queue and a jay than is normal in a woman of her age. She has been keeping a cumulative score for the last twenty years or so and her score now has so many noughts in it we have to use wider paper. She is a lesson to us all – all you have to do to win at Scrabble is to be so old and doddery that no one argues with you when you put pqzxyhgj across both triples, using up all your letters (apparently it is a breed of coelacanth found only in a single tributary of the Amazon).

Jan 9

I'm getting quite used to this blogging lark now and don't have to get up a minute before 3.30
a.m. to get it ready for my reader. Hello, Trevor, by the way – thanks for dropping by. I daresay by the end of the year I will be rolling it out without a second thought. Of course, I would choose this year to begin – there is an extra day to contend with, but I'll try to manage the extra workload – I have been a teacher for ever, so extra workload means nothing to me!

I have to concede that William Pitt (the Younger, that is and no, Seven Aitch Kay, no relation at all to Brad) was a pretty good Prime Minister, but God rot him for doing what he did on this day in 1799. He introduced income tax! To be fair, it was only levied on the rich and was only temporary until Napoleon was defeated, but that's not the point. He put the *idea* into the minds of government and now they soak everybody with it. Thanks a bunch, Master Billy!

In other news ... Apparently, Rudolf Bing was born on this day in 1902. He was an Austrian-born conductor and founded the Edinburgh Festival. But I don't really care about that – I just love the name. Put a 'Sir' on the front (which they did) and it sounds even better. When lots of people were trying to get his attention, it must have sounded like a scene from a submarine drama. Bing! Bing! Bing! Bing!

Jan 10

Living as we do in leafy Leighford, we rarely take the Tube, but of course it offers huge scope for losing the odd child on school trips to sundry museums; and, strangely, it always is the very oddest child that you do lose. But just out of interest, the Metropolitan Line opened in London today in 1863. Not only were we the first railway nation, we were the first underground railway nation too. The idea was to clear congestion in the capital's streets. Where did it all go wrong? Boris – any ideas?

> **References to Boris in 2012, of course, refer to him as Mayor of London, not Mayor of the whole UK, but it seems churlish to alter it and I can't remember the name of the ineffectual bloke who is actually Mayor of London today (Or should that be, I Khan remember?).**

In other news ... I was going to say something pithy and meaningful on the fact that eighty-four years ago women on both sides of the Atlantic got the vote. Then I took one look at my lovely better half pumping iron in the kitchen and thought better of it. Except to say ... jolly good; about time too!

Jan 11

On this day in 1569, the first ever lottery was held in England, with tickets on sale at the door of St Paul's Cathedral in London. You can't get there now for the tents of the anti-capitalist protesters who are no doubt mightily miffed they haven't won the lottery yet. By the way, in 1569 the first prize was a night out with the Queen's First Minister, Lord Burleigh. The second prize was two nights out with him.

Look – do you mind? That wasn't an old joke in 1569.

> **I understand that the anti-capitalise tents have now gone, but that members of Extinction Rebellion have glued their members to the walls of St Paul's.**

In other news ... Charing Cross railway station opened today in 1864. They used to have a bloke to sweep the horse s**t away so that ladies' skirts didn't drag through it on their way in.

In Boris Johnson's London today **(see above)**, you need a university degree to do that job and it only operates on alternate Thursdays due to health and safety regulations. I'm surprised that more people don't ride horses in London nowadays, though I may have missed the clause which states that they too are subject to the congestion charge.

Jan 12

Dear old Agatha Christie, the 'queen of crime' died today in 1976. I held a moment's silence in the Staff Room at the time but it was marred by some idiot (I think the Deputy Head) shouting 'The Mousetrap – the policeman did it!'

Can we just clear up her famous 'missing weekend' in 1926? She appeared in a hotel in Harrogate with no recollection of where she'd been. I've been to Harrogate on many occasions and it has happened to me every time. And anyway, the 'queen of crime' is clearly Mrs Detective Inspector Jacquie Carpenter-Maxwell, although to be honest if she wants to become a household name, I think she needs to make it something that trips off the tongue with a little more alacrity.

In other news ... Jack London was born today in 1876 (exactly a century before Agatha died – spooky, or what?). I've always had a soft spot for Jack. He not only captured the great outdoors of Canada and the US brilliantly in *White Fang* and *Call of the Wild*, his *People of the Abyss* about the Whitechapel ghetto a few years after Jack the Ripper, has never been bettered. Nobody wrote about London like London.

Jan 13

If you're as old as me (368) you'll remember Hugh O'Brien on the telly in a half hour show – they were all half an hour in the good old days when we apparently all had the concentration span of goldfish – as Marshal Wyatt Earp. The real guy died this day in 1929 and he's a fascinating character – played by Burt Lancaster, Henry Fonda, Kevin Costner and James Garner apart from O'Brien – with a moustache to die for. As a kid we all rooted for him at the gunfight at the OK Corral and just knew those Clantons and McLowerys were thoroughgoing baddies. I even had – and, thanks to the eBay watching proclivities of my good lady, have again – a replica Buntline Special Colt .45, Wyatt's purpose-built long-barrelled revolver. When I grew up of course I realized that Earp was a rather oily character, liar, gambler and cheat. That's what being an historian does for you. Life was so much simpler when we were kids, wasn't it?

In other news ... The Liverpool band known as the Beatles did quite well in the US pop charts this week in 1964, getting to a heady Number 45 with *I Wanna Hold Your Hand. Billboard* magazine said the track was 'a driving rocker with surf on the Thames sand'. I didn't understand that at the time and I still don't understand it now.

And finally – I don't know why I have written this blog for today; since, as it is Friday 13th, everyone is hiding under their beds until it is all over.

Jan 14

This is the day of infamy when the French President, Charles de Gaulle, said 'Non' (No) to
Britain's grovelling request to be allowed to join the European Economic Community (EEC) forerunner of the European Union (EU) and at the time usually referred to as the Common Market. In 1963, this was outrage. After all, Britain had put him up – and put up with him – during the war and won his country back for him in 1944. What an appalling act of ingratitude everybody except de Gaulle said – and they were right.

On reflection of course, he was trying to be helpful, we all now realise, having a pretty good prescience of what a petit dejeuner du chien the EU has become today.

In other news ... The Covent Garden Opera House re-opened after extensive renovation in 1947 and the show they opened with was *Carmen.* The whole thing was based on an old joke made popular by dear old Kenneth Horne in the 1960s –

'Carmen to the garden, Maud.' To which the reply was, 'Not just now; I'm Bizet.' They just don't sing them like that any more!

Jan 15

This was the day, 222 years ago, that Fletcher Christian and other mutineers from the Bounty landed at the uncharted Pitcairn Island in the South Pacific. Thanks to Hollywood – specifically Clark Gable, Marlon Brando and Mel Gibson – most people see Christian as a hero, striking a blow for the ordinary seaman against the tyranny, not to say psychopathy of Captain William Bligh – specifically Charles Laughton, Trevor Howard and Anthony Hopkins.

The real Bligh was a fair man and a brilliant sailor, and it was Fletcher Christian who was unstable and fomented the mutiny on the Bounty. The exact circumstances of his death are unclear, but it's at least likely he was killed in a fight over a Tahitian woman. Bligh went on to become an Admiral. So there is a God.

In other news ... The End of Civilization As We Know It happened in 1971. The grand old LSD of British currency – that's pounds, shillings and pence if you're under fifty – was swept away to create decimalization, where everything is based on multiples of ten. All right, so the Romans would have approved, but for the Angles, Saxons, Jutes, Danes, Norwegians and Normans who invaded this great country of ours, it simply made no sense at all. It was all quite simple: L stands for pound (obviously); s for shilling (duh!); and d for penny – could it be any clearer? There were 20 shillings in a pound. Now you don't have to be a mathematical genius to work out that before 1971 you got 140 *more* pennies to the pound than you did afterwards. Did nobody notice we were being conned?

AND ... regrettably I have to break off this historical reverie to announce with deep sorrow, that Waterstone's Bookshop has finally abandoned its apostrophe. And thats a 'shame becaus'e apo'strophe's were all that kept this country afloat. Perhap's the

Twenty-Twelver's have been s'peaking s'ens'e all along! **(But of cour'se they hadn't – s'ee front cover)**

Jan 16

The silliest law in History was brought in in 1920 when America introduced the Volstead Act banning alcohol. In a country dragged down by Amendments to its Constitution, the 18th arguably brought more misery than anything else. Did it lessen alcohol consumption? No. Was it followed even by a minority of Americans? No. Did it add enormously to the boot-legging empire of gangsters like Al Capone? You betchya.

On a positive note however, it did give us Kevin Costner's *The Untouchables* which provided the best line in Prohibition Era gangster flicks. Having thrown a baddie off a skyscraper so that he crashes through the roof of a parked Chrysler on the tarmac far below, Costner (Eliot Ness) is asked 'Where's Nitti?' the man in question having been Frank 'the Enforcer' Nitti, long time pal of Capone. He replies, 'In the car.' Genius!

To get back to Volstead, though; what will they do next? Ban smoking in public places? Get, as I'm sure Eliot Ness used to say, real.

In other news ... And talking of baddies, Ivan IV (who made Al Capone look like a choirboy) was crowned Tsar in Russia in 1547. He was responsible for the deaths of thousands of his own people, including his son and was in many ways the creator of a vicious secret police who have continued right the way down to the KGB and whatever they call it today. To be fair to the man, we know from the exhumation of his body carried out in the 1960s that he suffered from a bone deformity which probably left him in agony most days.

Even so, Ivan, there was no need to be *quite* so tetchy.

Metternich, reading, as is his rather annoying habit, over my shoulder has fastened on the word 'vole'. His reading skills are at best rudimentary, although not at all bad for a cat, but I need to explain to him that there is no danger of voles being banned, so that he releases the grip he has on my left ear lobe in order

15

that I can get on with my day relatively unmaimed.

Jan 17

'Great God, this is an awful place!' Yes, they were the words I used when I came to interview at Leighford High all those years ago, but I was actually quoting Robert Falcon Scott, who got to the South Pole exactly 100 years ago today, only to find a little tent in the white wilderness with a Norwegian flag pinned to it. It had been placed there by Raold Amundsen, the month before.

How must Scott have felt? I would have comforted myself –

a) in the knowledge that Amundsen had cheated by using dog sleds and
b) at least I wasn't on the Titanic.

In other news ... The year is young, but I am sure that even so my loyal reader will have noticed that I am not a great cricket fan. As a spectator sport, it equates with watching paint dry, but I do have a little nostalgia for the sound of leather on willow and remember the great days when large, wheezing smokers and beer-drinkers strolled around English greens wearing whites. It was all so civilized, with a smattering of applause every now and again, slightly muffled by a cucumber sandwich or slice of seed cake. So, what went wrong? Well, in 1933 we killed it stone dead by using the 'bodyline' bowling tactic. Purists will disagree with me, but it was essentially an attempt by British bowlers to kill – or at least seriously maim – Australian bowlers. It took a while, but the result today is plain to see: American baseball caps (why?); more body armour than the gladiators wore; and a profusion of sweatshirts and colours that have turned the game into a circus. Dressed like that, they might just as well be playing darts.

Jan 18

The first edition of the Boy's Own Paper hit the newsstands

today in 1879. It was published by the Religious Tract Society and contained uplifting stories and tales of derring-do. It couldn't be published today because: -

- It has an apostrophe in its title - (see Jan 15).
- The Religious Tract Society isn't the great publishing phenomenon it once was.
- Such things are only available on Kindle.
- Boys can't read - even Nolan has been known to listen to a download of his set text (currently *Fantastic Mr Fox*) rather than read the original. He is definitely a chip, but not necessarily off this old block in this particular.
- Nobody knows what derring-do actually is. A quick *vox pop* around my top set in Year Seven came up with 'that magician bloke off of the telly'.

Did you see what I did just then, by the way? Apparently, that is a bulletted list and the latest in my journey towards complete control of the world of cyber. Mrs B will be so proud. I found it rather difficult to stop doing them, rather like when someone teaches you to ride a bike, they never tell you how to stop without falling over sideways into some nettles.

In other news ... James Cook came across a group of islands in the Pacific 234 years ago today which the locals called Hawaii. The locals didn't like Cook very much - except perhaps as a light snack, as they eventually killed and, according to an inaccurate legend, ate him - probably because he called their land the Sandwich Islands. I should explain - because everyone has now forgotten - that this was in honour of the Earl of Sandwich, Comptroller (Big Cheese) of the Navy and not because of the snack thing mentioned earlier. Aloha!

Jan 19

Robert E Lee was born today in 1807. He was a gentleman and one of the finest generals any country has produced. Abhorrent though slavery was, several men who fought for the South in the

17

American Civil War didn't own slaves and didn't themselves approve. They were fighting for other causes, like state rights against the centralizing tyranny of Washington. Everybody, on both sides, treated Lee with respect and a way of life came to an end when he surrendered to General Grant at Appomattox Court House in April 1865. His last words, years later on his death bed were 'Strike the tents!' How cool is that?

In other news ... Many of you will know that I am a dedicated cyclist. White Surrey and I have rattled along more West Sussex roads than you've had parking tickets and so I say 'Huzzah!' in remembrance of this day in 1903 when the first Tour de France was contested. It was journalist Henri Desgrange's idea that sixty blokes would pedal like maniacs for 3,000 miles from Paris to Marseilles and back again. It was to be done in six steps over three weeks. I reckon Surrey and I could do it in two hours thirty. Oh, all right then, two hours thirty-eight, allowing for the head wind.

By the way, there was no Lycra in 1903; heady days.

Jan 20

Edwin 'Buzz' Aldrin was born 82 years ago today. He was 39 when he walked on the moon and everybody who knows him says what a great guy he is. He'll go down in history as the second man on the moon. Hence the unkind phrase 'You show me a silver medallist and I'll show you Buzz Aldrin'. Apparently, he doesn't believe in Global Warming – excellent! In my book, he's just gone from silver to pure gold.

In other news ... Today in 1265 the first ever meeting took place in Westminster Hall of what we might loosely call Parliament. Representatives from the Lords and Commons got together on the orders of Simon de Montfort, Earl of Leicester. Was this the start of democracy? No, because 'Commons' actually meant gentry (landowners) so something like 93 per cent of the country wasn't represented at all. Women of course didn't count. Neither did serfs.

But at least there were no outrageous claims for expenses

concerning second castles or falcon houses. So de Montfort had got something right. And just a note for Chanelle of Nine Tee Why; the word is serf, not smurf, and it has absolutely nothing to do with Mel Gibson painting his face blue in *Braveheart*. Well done for noticing it though, Chanelle, even if the logic is a little flawed.

> **If Simon de Montfort had lived to see what a complete Horlicks parliament made of the Brexit fiasco, he wouldn't have bothered.**

Jan 21

On this day in 1878, James Whistler (he of the Mother) sued the art critic John Ruskin in a libel action because Ruskin accused Whistler of 'flinging a pot of paint in the public's face'. Whistler got one farthing (that is a quarter of an old penny or one nine hundred and sixtieth of a pound to you, young reader) but that's not the point. Why did anybody listen to anything Ruskin said? After all, he was astonished to find that women had pubic hair and thought that J.M.W. Turner was a halfway decent painter. I should add here that my lovely wife is somewhat of a fan of JMWT and so if she sees this it may turn out to be my very last blog. Fortunately for me, I didn't realize her fondness for the man until she had moved in and it was too late – her *Fighting Temeraire* tea towel came as a bit of a shock at the time though, I don't mind telling you.

In other news ... It was a grim day for the British army 133 years ago today when the 24th Foot was wiped out by a force of Zulu Impis at Isandlwana. This was one of the worst defeats on record of a British force and modern attempts to explain it away include a) the Zulus were cheating because they took drugs to hype them up b) the British couldn't open their ammunition boxes because they were short of screwdrivers c) the smoke from their Lee Enfield rifles blinded them. The real reason was two-fold – a) the Zulus outnumbered the British three to one and b) the British commander, Lord Chelmsford, was an idiot. 'Nuff said.

For those disappointed that my computer skills seem to be worsening, then I would remind you that the bullet points of some days ago were by way of being a fluke. A's and B's were good enough for my old grandpappy and they are good enough for me.

Jan 22

In his diary entry for this day in 1924, George V wrote, 'Today 23 years ago dear Grandmama [that's Queen Victoria to you and me] died. I wonder what she would have made of a Labour government.'

What indeed? She might have been quite tickled that the new Prime Minister was Ramsay MacDonald, a crofter's son from the Heelands, a part of the country she adored. On the other hand, she is on record as saying that Irish terrorists should be lynched and women campaigning for the vote should be horse-whipped, so who knows?

I'm not sure she'd have gone a bundle on *Mrs Brown* (1997) or *Victoria and Abdul* (2017) either – the woman was *so* difficult to please.

In other news ... Time for another 'Bloody Sunday'. This was the third or fourth given that name and it happened in St Petersburg 107 years ago. about 1,000 people marched to the Winter Palace to protest to the Tsar, Nicholas II, about the appalling conditions in his country. They were led by Father Gapon who was himself a government spy. They were all unarmed and carried icons and portraits of Nicholas who they saw as their father. A panicky Guard commander ordered his troops to open fire and the blood of at least half the crowd stained the snow. The irony of all this? Nicholas wasn't even there.

Jan 23

Wasn't the Cold War great? Anybody under thirty must be

totally bewildered by spies coming in from the cold. They've had to create ever more unlikely baddies for James Bond to fight because the 'evil empire' is no more. Today in 1963, Kim Philby, the 'third man' disappeared in Beirut. He was the 'third man' because the 'first man' was Guy Burgess and the 'second man' was Donald Maclean (I hope you're following this because I *will* be asking questions later). MIs 5 and 6 were full of men, mostly recruited from Cambridge and often leaning to the left.

Personally, I thought Orson Welles' version of Philby was near perfect and what he could do with a zither could make your eyes water. Or have I got that wrong? These spies are very tricky people, as I am sure you know.

Today, most of them wander through Salisbury, the Casablanca of the Home Counties, smearing nasty stuff on people's doorknobs.

In other news ... There are some things you just shouldn't promise. Especially if you can't deliver; every parent who has ever let their attention wander as Christmas approaches knows this. Sometimes broken promises are bigger than those involving   a newbikeanahamsteranatigerarealtigernotatoyonelikelastyearand a ... we've all broken that one or something like it, usually inadvertently, but take as cases in point Marshal Ney, who promised to bring Napoleon back to Paris in a cage; in fact, he defected to him. Adolf Hitler promised not to invade any more countries just before he went into the Sudetenland, Czechoslovakia, Poland, Russia etc etc. But the most spectacular of all was Salvador Dali, the surrealist painter. 'Geniuses don't die,' he said. 'I'm going to live forever.' Except he didn't, dying today in 1989.

Who knew?

Jan 24

On this day in 1639 the settlers in Hartford, Connecticut voted for the Fundamental Orders, a constitution which gave them the right to set up a parliament and raise their own taxes. It didn't happen for a while of course because Connecticut actually belonged to the British crown. If the politicians in Britain had thought about it for a while, they wouldn't have made such a fuss. Did we really want, as part of our Empire, people who couldn't spell Hertford?

In other news ... Wilhelm Schouten, the Dutch navigator, sailed his ship around the treacherous tip of South America 396 years ago today. It had already been sighted, but not sailed around, by the Englishman Walter Ralegh and the Portuguese Ferdinand Magellan. Schouten named it Cape Hoorn after his birthplace in Holland. Thank God he wasn't born in Wijk bij Duurstede.

Jan 25

In 1980, the 'Gang of Four' came into being. No, not the Chinese counterrevolutionaries of the same name, but a rather more benign quartet – David Owen, Shirley Williams, Roy Jenkins and Bill Rodgers. They broke away from the Labour Party and formed the Social Democrats, which to those of us with an historical bent sounded like something out of the German Weimar Republic back in the Twenties. They spent most of their time deciding exactly what their party should be called so that today we have that august and impressive body known as the Lib-Dems. **For a reader born after 2001, that used to by a political party run by the Cable guy.**
Well done, chaps!

In other news ... Al Capone died today in 1947. As mobsters go, he was right up there with Paul Muni, Robert de Niro, Neville Brand, Jimmy Cagney, Humphrey Bogart, George Raft, Tom Hanks and Johnny Depp. At the height of his power he ran a vast bootlegging empire based in Chicago and is reckoned to have earned $105 million in 1927 alone (more or less my annual teacher's salary). By the time of his death, he had nothing and had done eleven years in prison for tax evasion.
So crime doesn't pay, then. Unless you're a taxman.

Jan 26

Let me take you back to a magic time. It was 26 January 1978 and technical staff at the EMI record company refused to press a disc of the Buzzcocks because they found the B side offensive. I don't know why they didn't find the A side offensive too, but I was probably out of step with the music world even then. I was more your Doris Day, Rosemary Clooney, Jim Reeves kind of guy. Even Cliff Richard was a little risque ...

In other news ... If you read the blog of yesterday, you'll know that Al Capone passed away in 1947. In 1973 screen bad guy Edward G Robinson made his exit stage left as well. 'Mother of God, is this the end of Edward G Robinson?' I rather liked the way he went in *Soylent Green*, being quietly euthanised to Beethoven's Pastoral. He'd probably have preferred a hail of bullets, but you can't have everything.

Some days in history just don't have much happening. January 26 is like one of those days from childhood when you were staying with your Granny. You know, the one you didn't see much of, the one with the moustache, the funny eye and that rather distressing smell you couldn't quite identify. It was just a day like any other, but it seemed longer and when it was over, you couldn't quite understand what it was all about and what you had done in it. That day was probably 26 January.

Jan 27

I shouldn't mock the afflicted but let me tell you a true tale of Seven Zed Ess. They were a lively bunch of individuals, prone to syndromes and disorders and we were doing a project on World War One. We did the trenches and the gas and tanks and in case the girls felt left out I let them do a project of their choice, but it had to be World War One related. Little Zephaniah (not his real name) chose a man who died on this day in 1989. He was Thomas Octave Sopwith. Zephaniah didn't find his middle name funny because he only had a slim grasp of music. What he found riveting about Sopwith is not only that he designed World War One aircraft but he was also the inventor of camels and puppies.

Today, I am proud to tell you that Zephaniah is Regius Professor of History at Oxford University (not its real name).

And today I am able to add that he wants to put up a *second* statue of Cecil Rhodes in that august city. Way to go, Zepaniah!

In other news ... It was on this day in 1868 that the journalist and explorer Henry Morton Stanley found the missing explorer (who was not a journalist) Dr Livingstone. His famous greeting of 'Dr Livingstone, I presume?' had endless comic possibilities. He could have said 'No' and then where would we be? He could have said 'Yes, but you'll have to make an appointment at Reception.' In fact, he missed the moment and just said 'Aye' or something suitably Scottish.

Incidentally, Livingstone wasn't missing. He knew exactly where he was all the time.

Jan 28

A lot of people assume that the drug culture is a late twentieth century phenomenon tied in with rock and roll, easy sex and young people. As an historian I can refute that. If you had the cash, the hard stuff has been available for much longer. For instance, it is on record that on this day in 1817, the Prince Regent was stoned in St James's Park.

In other news ... The Irish poet W.B. Years died today in 1939. As he himself nearly wrote in one of his best-known poems, 'A terrible beauty is dead.'

This Saturday the Maxwell family is taking itself off up to London for the day. Mrs Maxwell – or Detective Inspector Carpenter-Maxwell to give her her full title – occasionally gets a hankering for the bright lights and so we head northish and a tiny bit eastish and hit the Great Wen. Nolan is becoming quite the city slicker these days and thinks nothing of hailing a taxi. The trick now is to stop him hailing a taxi without asking first; it is quite a heart stopping experience to see one's only son disappearing down Regent Street in the back of a black cab. The cabbies like him though – he's a heavy tipper.

Jan 29

Alan Ladd died 48 years ago today. Impossibly good looking, the actor had to endure endless Hollywood jokes about his height. When he was standing alongside other actors, the cameras had to be angled just *so*. When he was kissing his leading lady, he was on a box or she was in a trench and he needed a stepladder to mount his horse. I don't care if some or all these stories are true, he was the star of the greatest Western film ever made – *Shane* – and at least Ladd's death on this day ended the old chestnut. Did Alan Ladd die at the end of *Shane*? No, he lived on, riding into the sunset, for another eleven years!

In other news ... On this day in 1978, Sweden banned the use of aerosol sprays on the grounds that they were destroying the ozone layer. Can I just stick my sixpenn'orth in here?
* There is no such thing as global warming
* If there is, it has happened throughout history and has nothing to do with man
* Since 1978 Swedes have become very smelly indeed (as opposed to parsnips, which have retained their delightful natural fragrance)

Bullet points are back on the menu, but purely by accident. Don't get used to what you may perceive as a bold new cyber-savvy Peter Maxwell because he doesn't exist! Dinosaurs-R-Us.

You will also notice that I have forborne to mention the old joke about the Swede who goes into a chemist looking for a deodorant. It is a classic, but it needs the accent to tell it well – you'll just have to imagine it.

Not heard it? Okay then – the shopkeeper says 'Bol or aresol?' And he says (still in Swedish accent) 'Neither, I want it for my armpits.' You see, I told you it had to be in the accent!

Jan 30

If you go to Carisbrooke Castle in the Isle of Wight, you'll find a little chapel there, dedicated to the martyrdom of King Charles I. Not many people regard him as a martyr, even though they chopped his head off outside his own palace at Whitehall 363 years ago today (Incidentally, they've changed the calendar since then so this figure may not be totally accurate). Whatever Charles was deemed to have done – ruled without parliament, raised taxes without their consent, married a Catholic wife etc etc) the trial itself was illegal, presided over by a foreign judge. The jury was not made up of Charles's peers (i.e. his equals – twelve other kings) and the usual rules of evidence were waived. Having supposedly caused the deaths of thousands of his countrymen in the civil war, he was replaced by Oliver Cromwell who proceeded to do exactly the same thing in Scotland and Ireland. Historians, of course, know this already – and can point to almost any regime change where the body count is actually higher afterwards than before. Try it – you'll find it is horribly difficult to find any example which disproves that statement.

In other news ... Anton Chekov, the Russian playwright was born this day in 1860. His plays include *The Seagull* and *The Cherry Orchard* and his grandson, Pavel Chekov, went on to become the little guy with the irritating and unconvincing Russian accent under James T. Kirk on the Enterprise.

Jan 31

On this day in 1835 a national sport was started called Shooting the President. It is now carried out on a regular basis, providing endless work for conspiracy theorists, secret service agents, journalists, Lee Harvey Oswald lookalikes and JFK deniers.

The first round of the game featured 'Old Hickory' Andrew Jackson (you may remember Charlton Heston played him in *The Buccaneer*) as the target of house-painter Richard Lawrence as the assassin. Lawrence may have been a few bullets short of a murder attempt for two reasons. Firstly, his gun jammed and secondly, he claimed to be the rightful king of England, which came as something of a surprise to William IV, who actually was. What Lawrence didn't know was that Jackson already carried two lead slugs in his body from duels fought over gambling debts.

Why don't they make Presidents like that any more – although having said that, it would be pointless, since Charlton Heston is no longer around to play them on film!

In other news ... Most accounts will tell you that 'mild mannered murderer' H.H. Crippen poisoned his wife, Belle Elmore, and partially dismembered her body before stashing it in the cellar of their house at 63, Hilldrop Crescent on this day in 1910. Who said so? Chief Inspector Walter Dew of Scotland Yard. On what evidence? On the say-so of the pathologist Bernard Spilsbury, whose God-like reputation was created by this case.

Unfortunately, the remains in the cellar were those of a man. Oops – nice one, Dr Spilsbury. **(And, by the way, the remains do not match the DNA of *any* of Belle's family.)** That doesn't mean of course that Crippen didn't kill Belle Elmore and it might mean that he also killed the anonymous bloke in the cellar. What it *does* mean, however, is that there is no hard evidence that Crippen killed anybody. A posthumous pardon is long overdue and when *is* Belle Elmore going to come forward? At the very least, DCI Dew's famous book (1935) should be retitled *I Caught an Innocent Man (Probably)*.

FEBRUARY

Feb 1

American heart throb Clark Gable was born today in 1901, the same day, coincidentally, that Queen Victoria died. Conspiracy theorists are sure there is a plot involved somewhere, but as I write, they are not sure what – give them time, they'll come up with something eventually.

It may be that I'm too male and too young to appreciate Gable, but I never quite took to him. Those huge ears, that silly moustache and an essential inability to act, should have precluded him from Hollywood stardom. Apparently, he had bad breath as well, but that was really just an issue between him and his leading lady. Incidentally, did you know that his famous last line of *Gone With The Wind* (the most over-rated film in history apart from, arguably, *The Sound of Music*) was originally 'Frankly, my dear, I don't really care.'

Well done to whoever insisted on changing that – although it didn't amount to a hill of beans as regards improving the film.

In other news … Seventy years ago today, Vidkun Quisling became Prime Minister of Norway under German occupation. So detested was he, at home and abroad, that his name became synonymous with treachery and traitorous behaviour. So, if you really want to offend someone, all you have to do is say 'You Vidkun,' and watch them react with horror.

Feb 2

New Amsterdam became New York today in 1665. The British drove out the Dutch settlers who had bought Manhattan from the Native Americans for a broken mirror and a pack of Hula Hoops and were led by their thoroughly unpleasant chain-smoking Governor Peter Stuyvesant (he of the silver leg – what a terrible birth defect). Stuyvesant was a rabid Puritan who imprisoned people for playing tennis (actually, not a bad idea) and no one was sorry to see him go.

Song lyric writers of course are particularly grateful. Imagine getting your tongue and guitar chords around 'New Amsterdam, New Amsterdam' – so good they renamed it.

In other news ... One of the all-time survivors of History was born 258 years ago today. His name was Charles Maurice de Talleyrand-Perigord and as you've probably guessed, he was of the French persuasion. As an aristocrat, he became adviser to Louis XVI, he of the less-than-happy encounter with Madame Guillotine, but bounced back to become adviser to the Revolutionary Government. When Napoleon Bonaparte seized power, who should be at his elbow but Talleyrand and when the Emperor was defeated at Waterloo, b****r me, he's there again, giving sound and sensible advice to his successor, Louis XVIII.

I don't know if you've noticed the occasional PR presentation by Barack Obama from the White House, but there's a little old boy with a wig and breeches in the background who I can't help but think looks a little familiar ...

Since that snapshot of history, the Viscomte has been no-platformed by President Trump for looking at him funny.

Feb 3

Old time-honoured Gaunt, father of Henry IV, popped his sollerets today in 1399. I've always felt a bit sorry for this guy, what with the peasants being revolting enough to tear down his palace at the Savoy in 1381 and nobody being able to pronounce his name properly – it was actually Ghent, of course. Richard II also gave him a hard time and even when Gaunt's little boy became Henry IV, his reign was plagued by wars and rebellions. Which just goes to show that money, land, palaces, titles and getting a starring role in Shakespeare can't buy you happiness.

In other news ... Thirty-three years ago today, Yasser Arafat became leader of the PLO. A Head of Music at Leighford, now moved on to higher things – I believe he busks in Notting Hill most Saturdays – could never understand why so many people did as they were told by the erstwhile conductor of the Plymouth

Light Orchestra.

It is looking as though Nolan might be going to be musical, one of those strange genetic quirks that sometimes happens. I for example can tell two tunes apart, if someone stands in front of me and shouts the name of one of them very loudly and repeatedly, while smacking me round the head. My good lady can tell all kinds of tunes one from another and can sing after a fashion. I wish instead of singing she would stop the shouty person coming into the house while I am trying to listen to music, though. But Nolan has the voice of an angel and is being taught the recorder by Mrs Troubridge; fortunately for Metternich's temper, the lessons take place chez Troubridge.

Feb 4

There was outrage today in Vienna back in 1928 because of the naughty stage act of Josephine Baker. The forerunner in many ways of Rihanna and Lady Gaga by way of Madonna, 'Hot Jazz' Josephine upset Viennese Nazis because of her skimpy banana skin costume. Apparently, it upset them because it was indecency in public. Actually of course it showed far too much of her dark skin for their liking and must have upset their delicate Aryan sensibilities. Six years later, they let Adolf Hitler in.

In other news ... Back in 1861 the greatest nation on earth (according to some definitions) almost destroyed itself by an illegal opt-out clause. On this day, seven of the soon-to-be Disunited States met in Montgomery, Alabama (curiously, named after a British general who hadn't been born yet) and agreed to set up the Confederate States of America. Apart from causing the deaths of more Americans than in any of their conflicts before or since, it produced some worthless currency, rather nice French grey uniforms, a plethora of Southern Belles, some great marching tunes and one of the worst films ever made - *Gone With the Wind.*
Thanks, guys.

And by the way, the list of girl (and rather mature lady, in the case of Madonna) singers above is courtesy of the boys of Eleven Emm Oh. So please be reassured that the sentence represents their tastes, not mine! I am more an Enya or Hayley Westenra kind of chap. I particularly liked Hayley's performance in Bram Stoker's *Dracula*.

Feb 5

George Orwell's Big Brother hit Mayfair today in 1958. Robot-like machines called Parking Meters were installed on pavements to make life just that *bit* more unbearable for motorists and the Greater London Council just that *bit* richer. The Americans had been doing this in some cities since 1935 but that's no excuse. This was soon followed of course by Traffic Wardens who were called Little Hitlers for obvious reasons (they all had small toothbrush moustaches and had failed to get into Art College).

Clobbering the motorist has been a national (and especially a London) sport ever since.

In other news ... The year before parking meters, Bill Haley and the Comets arrived in London to the delight of squealing fans and to the horror of the Establishment. If you ever see footage of this Rock 'n' Roll invasion, check out (as you young people say) the extraordinary banality of it all. Bill looks well over fifty, is an unsexy chubby bloke in a shiny grey suit and has what my mother's generation called a 'kiss curl' on his forehead. Benjamin Disraeli had one too, but his band – the Conservative Party – had nothing like the success of Bill Haley. A pre-Rock 'n' Roll generation were perfectly happy with hit numbers like 'Won't you go home, Bill Haley, won't you go home?' They don't write 'em like that any more.

I feel at this point that I need to set a record straight. When the Year Sevens arrive at Leighford High School every September, bright eyed and bushy tailed before the enthusiasm gets knocked out of them, I let them guess my age. Although not a man with a mathematical bent, as my friend can attest, I have kept a rough running total and every now and again work out my actual age against my Year Seven Age. There is probably some formula, like AA* x YSA** + fo**** = YACF*****/infinity which would help me work it out, but basically, I am around 563, according to Year Seven. Not bad, but no cigar. Not even behind the bike sheds.

* Actual Age
** Year Seven Age
**** number of times
I get sworn at by Year
Seven
***** Years at Chalk
Face.

Feb 6

Kit Marlowe was born today in 1564 in the parish of St George in Canterbury. His dad was a tanner and shoemaker and Kit was a bright boy who sang beautifully, studied the Classics at the King's School and went on to Corpus Christi College, Cambridge, where he started to write naughty poetry (based on Ovid) and do a bit of spying on the side for Sir Francis Walsingham, the 'M' of his day. How did it all turn out? The history books will tell you that he died in a tavern brawl in Deptford in 1593, but since he changed his name to William Shakespeare and became the greatest playwright of all time, *that* can't be right!

In other news ... Joseph Priestley died today in 1804. He discovered (not invented, despite the contentions of Seven Eff Pea) oxygen and was a Radical politician whose house was burnt down by a right-wing mob who didn't care for his views on the French Revolution – which he believed was the best thing since sliced bread ... which he also didn't invent.

In later years, he used his initials JB and became a successful writer (only joking, Seven Eff Pea).

Feb 7

This was the birthday 142 years ago today, of the psychoanalyst Alfred Adler. His mother was Irene, with whom Sherlock Holmes had a 'thing' and of course his dad was Larry, the harmonica player. Alfred himself came up with the idea of the inferiority complex, but he didn't want to make a fuss about it.

In other news ... On this day in 1886 a carpenter called George Walker found gold in the Transvaal in South Africa whilst building a cottage. The Boers (Dutch farmers who had settled there years earlier) were concerned that thousands of trouble-making foreigners would swarm into the area which I would imagine was exactly the same thing that the Zulus had feared when the Boers had arrived.

Feb 8

'A dead woman bites not' said Lord Grey with astonishing perspicacity. He was talking about Mary Stuart, Queen of Scots, a pleasant enough woman who was never known to have bitten anybody, even when alive. She was beheaded on this day in 1587 at the castle of Fotheringhay (now a ruin) on the reluctant orders of her cousin, Elizabeth Tudor, Queen of England. The two never met, despite that scene in the film where Vanessa Redgrave and Glenda Jackson have a go at each other with riding crops and Elizabeth instantly regretted having it done. What did it achieve? Nothing. The Stuarts got the throne of England after all, giving rise to Ramsay MacDonald, Tony Blair, Gordon Brown, **Nicola Sturgeon** and the West Lothian Question. Who knew?

In other news ... The Boy Scouts of America was founded today in 1910, along the lines of the British movement of two years earlier set up by Colonel Robert Baden Powell, the hero of Mafeking. Isn't it a pity that his book *Scouting for Boys* is so widely misunderstood today and that mafeking is strictly contrary to EU regulations?

On the other hand, the Colonel's penchant for wearing rather fetching day dresses is widely accepted now on both sides of the Atlantic, drag though it is.

Feb 9

It was 9 February 1964 when 73 million viewers watched the Beatles on the Ed Sullivan Show. They proceeded to take the good ol' USA by storm, although I've never quite understood why. At the time, girls of all ages were swooning over the mop top four in Europe and I must say that even in the Maxwell household, not exactly a cutting edge sort of place musically, rang to the sounds of their music. When somebody asked John Lennon how he had found America, he replied, 'It's easy, you turn left at Greenland.' Now, who did he pinch that from?

In other news ... The Boxer Rebellion kicked off today in 1899 with pamphlets telling everybody how much the Chinese hated Europeans. The Boxers were actually called the Fists of Righteous Harmony and they were the forerunners of all those terrible Kung Fu/Martial Arts films of the 70s and 80s. European churches apparently, got in the way of Heaven; Christianity was disrespectful to the ancient Gods; and worst of all, Europeans' (barbarians') eyes were so disgustingly blue.

Nothing for the Commission for Racial Equality to get its knickers in a twist over there, then.

And in yet other news ... I have to include this third item because today in 1865 Mrs Patrick Campbell was born. She was the first Eliza Doolittle in Pygmalion and had a bit of a fling with George Bernard Shaw (she was obviously very short sighted). What I've never understood about her is a) what happened to Mr Patrick Campbell or b) why were her parents so cruel as to call her Patrick in the first place?

Feb 10

There was a touch of overkill 445 years ago today when a handful of miffed Scotsmen blew up Lord Darnley's house in Kirk o' Field, Edinburgh. Not content to blow him apart with gunpowder, the conspirators had strangled him too and left his body in the garden. Some said 'Serves him right' because he had orchestrated the murder, months earlier, of his wife's Italian secretary, David Riccio (I should perhaps point out at this juncture that his wife was Mary, Queen of Scots and she may have been having a bit of how is your father with Riccio). The secretary was stabbed to death in front of her..

It all makes Alex Salmond **(now known as Nicola Sturgeon)** and the SNP look rather tame, doesn't it?

In other news ... The great American comedian Jimmy Durante was born on this day in 1893. A wisecracking, fast-talking Vaudeville star, Durante was famous for his huge nose, known affectionately as his Schnoz. He's been gone for a while now of course, but my impeccable rendering of 'Goodnight, Mrs Calabash, wherever you are,' still has young Nolan rolling in the aisles.

Feb 11

Isn't it funny what a difference four centuries make? Today in 1858 a 14-year-old girl,
Bernadette Soubirous claimed to have seen the Virgin Mary eighteen times in a grotto at Lourdes in the Pyrenees. The Pope sent emissaries to check her out and even today the place is a holy shrine where believers go to soak up its spirituality.

Back in 1431, when another French teenager, Jeanne d'Arc, claimed to hear voices from God, the Papacy accused her of heresy and the English burned her at the stake.

That's what I like to see; consistency.

In other news ... An elderly aunt of mine was outraged today back in 1975 when Margaret Thatcher became the leader of the Conservative party. I was, frankly, surprised. Aunt Mathilde (not her real name) had been a suffragette, a flapper and a bra burner in her long and distinguished feminist career and I'd have thought she'd have been delighted to find the crusty old Tories (of all people) electing a woman to the top job. It was several weeks before I discovered why. Aunt Mathilde's eyesight wasn't what it had been, and she'd misread an editorial in one of the dailies. It said that Margaret Thatcher was a 'woman of strong conviction' but Auntie had read it as 'a woman with a string of convictions.'

Should've gone to Specsavers.

Feb 12

John Donne – pronounced Dun – the Dean of St Paul's, died today in 1631. After Shakespeare, Dickens, Wilde, Shaw, Marlowe, Sheridan and Enid Blyton, he is the most quoted writer in history. As I often say to Ten Aitch Dee, 'Never send to know for whom the school bell tolls; it may fall on thee.' My good lady, the Detective Inspector and I have a small and harmless hobby, of listening for John Donne quotes in unlikely situations. We think we have heard the ultimate now, so may have to rethink how we spend our leisure time. Out and about recently, Nolan, whose bladder is the size of a carrier bag when at home but a walnut when driving anywhere, needed a pee. We stopped at a peculiarly greasy cafe on the side of the road and because we are very polite people, bought something to eat and drink rather than just widdling and running. This may be why we have to stop so often of course – Nolan always seems to take in far more liquid than he gets rid of on these little pauses in our journey. Note to self – think about joining the thousands of people who let their kids wee on the hard shoulder ... Where was I? Yes, well, in this cafe there was suddenly a deafening crash as a tray full of crockery hit the deck and in the ringing silence which followed one voice, in a strong (and in a dark alley very menacing) Glaswegian voice said simply, 'No man is an island' and suddenly everybody rushed to help. Humanity is alive and well and driving a lorry somewhere in England.

In other news ... Back in 1831, J.W. Goodrich of Boston (Mass) invented the rubber galosh. Now, I'm quite intrigued by this. Did Mr Goodrich invent one galosh, intending it to become a international sport – 'Premier League Galoshing'? Or did he perhaps only have one leg (as Peter Cook and Dudley Moore, may they rest in peace, would have it, was he a unidexter) thereby not needing to waste yet more time on a second galosh?

Was he actually working on a revolutionary cloning technique at the same time so that he need ever only invent one galosh?

And when it comes right down to it, what is a galosh anyway? I am, frankly, at a galosh to explain it.

PS – I fully expect, dear Blog Follower, that galosh will now replace Stephen Fry's Garboldisham as the silliest word in the English language.

Feb 13

The massacre at Glencoe took place today in freezing conditions back in 1692. The Macdonald of that Ilk and thirty-six of his men were hacked to death by their house guests the Campbells. The official reason was that the Macdonalds had not signed an oath of allegiance to William III. In fact, they had, but severe precipitation in the Highlands had caused a delay. Now there are a number of interesting historical observations to be made about all this:

a) If you invite 129 armed Scotsmen to spend the night with you, don't go to sleep.

b) If you intend to have a massacre, you've got to do a bit better than thirty-seven casualties. Typical of the Scots to skimp on the crowd scenes, as the satirical magazine *Punch* once said.

c) This is the first recorded example of Be Nice to Oldies Week. The orders sent to the Campbell of *that* Ilk was that everybody under 70 was to be put to the sword. Everybody else could get their winter fuel allowance, bus passes and a Saga holiday in the Trossachs.

In other news ... Back in 1971, Spiro T Agnew, the American Vice President, hit three spectators with a golf ball while playing in the Bob Hope Desert Classic Tournament. Now, I wasn't there, so I'm entitled to enquire firstly, did these three volunteer, lining up for the privilege of being whacked by the Vice President? Sounds like a fine Good Ol' Boy custom. I would also like to know whether Mr Agnew took three swings with three balls and get lucky each time or was this a brilliant ricochet shot, that bounced off a palm tree, the three spectators one by one and then plop accurately into the hole?

If you have the answer, please keep it to yourself – and that goes double if you are one of the victims. After being struck on the head by a golf ball, I have grave doubts as to whether anything you say could be even slightly accurate.

Feb 14

Don't you just love saints' days? There are so many of them that nobody worked at all during the Middle Ages and the Industrial Revolution happened first in Britain because we didn't have any at all. Except St Valentine's Day. Now this is all rather odd because there are two possible Valentines after whom the day is named. One was an early Christian priest put to death in the reign of Claudius the Goth (you couldn't miss him – black hair, purple makeup, didn't like sunlight). The other one was the Bishop of Turin, executed in Rome in a similar clampdown against what was, after all, a heretical sect. Neither of these men had anything to do with Love, Hearts, Cupid or nauseatingly schmaltzy greetings cards, so work it out for yourselves. It may be that 14 February was seen as the start of the mating season, but this is a Family Blog so we won't pursue that.

All we can be sure of is that in Chicago in 1929 the day was celebrated by Al Capone shooting seven of 'Bugs' Moran's heavies in a garage on the North Side. Three of the five executioners wore police uniforms, though whether they were real cops or just Capone's people in fancy dress was open to doubt. Since half of Chicago's finest were under investigation for corruption at the time, you just couldn't be sure.

In other news ... Richard II died today in 1400. I've always felt rather sorry for this guy. He was high-handed, didn't like the Irish and popularized the use of:-

a) forks

b) handkerchiefs and

c) riding sidesaddle – for ladies of course; nothing 'funny' about Richard II.

He also had a cool heraldic badge – the White Hart (that's a deer to you, Seven Emm Eff) now famous as a pub sign throughout the civilized world. He was almost certainly murdered in Pontefract Castle (or Pomfret, as Shakespeare called it, thereby proving that England's greatest playwright was also dyslexic) on the orders of Henry IV (who later, as you'd expect, denied it).

Feb 15

Charles Tiffany was born today in 1812. It came as a bit of a surprise to Mrs Tiffany who was having breakfast at the time.*

*I think I remember the song.

In other news ... Somebody else born today (in 1748 in fact) was Jeremy Bentham, the radical philosopher who gave the world Utilitarianism. This basically means the greatest happiness of the greatest number when applied to politics, although the phrase itself was Joseph Priestley's and Bentham pinched it. He invented a sort of clapometer to measure happiness – the Felicific Calculus – but since he didn't know about, for example, sadism or masochism, his results were always going to be flawed.

He also founded University College London – the working man's college – and in his will insisted he be able to continue to watch over the students. I'm not sure if he's still there, but I remember seeing the great man in a glass case at the end of the main corridor. He's sitting on a chair with his thigh bones poking out of his worn breeches. His head is a wax copy, but the real one is in the hat box between his feet. The cleaners of course will tell you that every night, he gets up and has a stroll around the old place.

Yeah, as Nine Pee Pee would have it, right.

Feb 16

There were near riots today in 1939 when a new item of ladies' doo-dahs went on sale for the first time in the US of A. They were stockings, which had been around for centuries, but they were made of a new synthetic stuff called nylon. Stronger and sheerer than silk (and you don't need worms to make it) it's cheap and cheerful and much easier to wash and dry. It was patented two years earlier by the Du Pont Company and invented by W.H. Carothers who died soon afterwards. I don't mean any disrespect to Mr Carothers when I say that this was probably just as well or we'd have dodgy men sneaking into ladies' lingerie departments of big stores and asking for 'a pair of Carothers, please.' Doesn't sound quite right, does it?

In other news ... The first cheque was signed 353 years ago in England when Nicholas Vanacker wrote one to a creditor. The idea was to dispense with coinage as a letter of credit and to try to compete with the sophisticated Lombard banking system. Messrs Barclays announced just yesterday that Mr Vanacker's cheque should clear within the next five working days.

Feb 17

The Chiricahua Apache chief Geronimo died on this day in 1909. He fought the US cavalry for years in Arizona and New Mexico, breaking out of a reservation in 1876 and hitting the White Eyes for ten years in brilliant guerrilla raids. After that, he lived the American dream.

He may look a fierce old so-and-so in the photographs, glowering at the camera and brandishing his Sharp's rifle but as well as being a great general, he was a pretty s**t hot entrepreneur, selling Apache memorabilia and signing them with his name.

Incidentally, there is no truth in the rumour that he died during a sexual debauch by leaping off a wardrobe onto an unsuspecting lady, shouting 'Geronimo!'.

That was Rain-in-the-Face.

In other news ... In 1972 the German Volkswagen outsold the

US Ford Model T with sales of over 15 million. I've always found this rather odd – that a Nazi car with the engine in the wrong place should have been designed by a man who gave his name to an altogether more upmarket car with the engine in the right place.

You couldn't make it up, could you? Although Holocaust deniers do.

On a personal note, the Detective Inspector dislocated her elbow this week, sliding on an inadequately stowed vole innard in the garage. She and Metternich have kissed and made up, but my additional housewifely duties have caused a slight hiatus in the blog – normal service has been resumed, as you can see, but the cooking and housework will be in the capable hands of Mrs Troubridge from Monday when I return to school after half term, so I warn you in advance that some entries may be a little dyspeptic.

Feb 18

John Bunyan published the first part of his Pilgrim's Progress today in 1678. It was an allegory of man's journey from sin to salvation and boring as Hell. Some 'great' works have survived the passage of time – Chaucer's *Canterbury Tales*, quite a bit of Shakespeare, a line or two of Milton – because they really are great. Unfortunately, Bunyan had silly characters like Mr Worldly Wiseman and Giant Despair, making nonsense of the whole thing. His editors should have said to him, 'Needs work, Bunny, baby. Oh, and how's little Paul doing in the lumberjack business?'

In other news ... Clyde Tombaugh, American astronomer, discovered a new planet today in 1930. He called it Pluto after Mickey Mouse's dog and spent the next ten years looking for its moons, Donald, Huey, Dewey and Louie.

Feb 19

What is it with Iceland? Not content with sparking off a Cod

War on this day in 1976, they've done nothing but annoy people ever since. They extended their fishing grounds from three nautical miles to twelve in 1958 and to fifty in 1972. This was presumably because they'd caught all their fish and wanted somebody else's. They then sank two trawlers and rammed HMS *Andromeda*. This was only the start, however. More recently they've grounded aircraft all over the world with their volcanic smog, upset international finances with a banking collapse and given us a High Street shop that sells nothing but frozen food.

What have we got in return? Bjork.

I rest my case.

In other news ... A brilliant new gadget appeared in the skies over Paris ninety-one years ago today. It was a very light (220 lbs) aircraft with a 25-horsepower engine that drove two large rotating blades. It got off the ground all right and hovered, but landing was a bit of a b***h and no one could predict which direction it was going to go in.

The idea was sound, though – thank God somebody came up with a better name than the one its inventor hoped would take off – the Oehmichencopter.

Feb 20

As you know I am not of the driving persuasion, preferring my trusty old velocipede White Surrey for the school run. but my good lady wife is constantly fretting should a warning light appear on the car's dashboard. 'What's that? What's that?' she screams (as if I have an answer). Spare a thought, then, for John Glenn, who noticed a similar light on his dashboard on 20 February 1962. The only problem was that he was circling the earth at the time in his Friendship-7 capsule and couldn't get through to the AA (or AAA as he would doubtless call it). The flashing light meant that his heat shield was loose and the craft could have disintegrated as it hurtled back into the earth's atmosphere.

Luckily for Glenn all it actually meant was that Friendship 7 was due for its annual service, so no harm done.

Phew!

In other news ... The French philosopher Voltaire was born on this day in 1694. He upset a lot of Englishmen in his book, *Candide* in which he explains the execution of Admiral John Byng by saying that the English shoot an admiral every now and again to encourage the others. He saw himself as a campaigner against injustice and a champion of freedom. Everybody else saw him as a slimy cynic. But then, if you're a chap christened Francois Marie Arouet, you've got every right to be cynical.

Feb 21

To all friends of the Alamo, Davy Crockett, Jim Bowie etc, can I remind you that Antonio Lopez de Santa Anna was born on this day in 1794.

If you're not a friend of the above or have never heard of them (shame on you, Seven Are Why) the Alamo was a mission in San Antonio de Bexar, Texas which was defended by a handful of volunteers including Crockett, Bowie etc against General Santa Anna's army in 1836. Outnumbered and outgunned, the garrison was overrun after thirteen days and every man killed. Santa Anna had set his people free from the autocratic rule of Spain only to proclaim himself dictator.

If only people would use their sense. What else can you expect from someone whose first names are Tony the Wolf?

In other news ... The French playwright Moliere was buried 338 years ago today – or rather, tonight, because the whole thing was carried out secretly in the wee small hours and without a priest in attendance. Moliere was one of that select band of actors/artistes who have died on stage (see Tommy Cooper, Sid James) but he made enemies in the Church and at the court of Louis XIV.

Nowadays if playwrights are unpopular, people just don't go to see their stuff (*see ...., ..., ...).

*censored because of the laws of libel in this great country of ours.

Feb 22

Let's hear it for the Women of Mumbles Head – or at least, somewhere nearby – 212 years ago today, a French Frigate landed at Fishguard in Pembrokeshire.I should perhaps remind you of the following -

1. We were at war with France at the time.
2. The frigate's captain thought Wales was Ireland.
3. He was supposed to be linking up with a rebellion that had already failed weeks before.

That said, his men were mean, armed and determined to carry out a bit of rape and pillage which have been soldiers' R&R for centuries. Along the beach they saw people advancing with red coats and black headgear and said (to themselves and each other) 'Merde! C'est l'Infanterie de l'Angleterre!' (S**t! British squaddies!). They were wrong in fact because these were Welsh fishwives in their traditional red shawls and black hats. They were far more terrifying than the regular army and the French ran for it. The Pembrokeshire Yeomanry (that's part time cavalry to you, Eight Tee Tea) waited until the coast was clear (literally) then galloped up with lots of cries of 'Huzzah!' and had the battle honour 'Fishguard' put on their accoutrements (that's bits and bobs to you, Twelve Aitch Why).

In other news ... Jethro Tull died today in 1741. Nothing whatever to do with the 'music' industry, this was the guy who brought you such literary classics as *Horse-Howing Husbandry* (he was a stickler for alliteration) and *Essay on the Principles of Tillage and Vegetation*. Tull was not just a theorist, however; his horse-hoe really worked, as did his seed drill which planted seeds in neat rows, making a nonsense of the parable of the sower and ensuring that every seed planted actually grew. What was the response of farm labourers whose work was cut dramatically and whose families could now eat properly? They went on the rampage and smashed up Tull's machinery.

Ingrates!

Feb 23

It's one of those great photographs that have become legend – GIs erecting the stars and stripes on battle-torn Iwo-Jima on this day in 1945. Dear old Clint Eastwood in his recent film has blown the gaffe on this incident. and if you've seen the sequence of stills taken just before and after *that* one, they're very average, In the first one, the GIs are having difficulty lifting the flag in the high wind. In the later ones, job done, they're standing around having a fag! Eastwood revealed that the actual scene took place when there were no cameras around, so it had to be re-staged for the Press later.

Darn!

In other news ... Next time you're in the West End, find a quiet little Mews near Hyde Park called Cato Street. At one end of it, there's a house which was once a stable. It was here, on this day in 1820 that the revolutionary Arthur Thistlewood and his co-conspirators were caught making grenades before going to Lord Harrowby's house in nearby Grosvenor Square to blow up the entire Cabinet who were having dinner there.

The whole plot had been rumbled weeks earlier and the conspirators were arrested in the hayloft by the Bow Street Runners (precursors of Mrs Carpenter-Maxwell's profession) in which one of them was killed.

Had it come off, it would have been the boldest and most devastating political coup in British history. Except that Arthur Thistlewood was probably mad as a tree and seems to have had no real plan as to what to do had the plot worked.

Feb 24

You know it's the fashion nowadays for some parents to name their kids after the place they were conceived – Brooklyn Beckham, Chelsea United, Washington Irving for example. Well, on this day in 1920, Nancy Astor went one further. This was the day that a woman (other than Victoria) spoke for the first time in the Houses of Parliament. I'm not commemorating the day here, but her husband's name – Waldorf Astor – conceived, no doubt, in the hotel (or salad) of the same name. I can only assume that this is the origin of the name of my bête noire in Year Nine, Premier Travelodge Johnson.

In other news ... Five hundred and thirty years ago today (give or take eleven days) Pope Gregory XIII introduced the Gregorian calendar to replace the Julian one. All very confusing, in which days are lost or gained based on a book (the Old Testament) that makes no chronological sense at all. Logic? 365 days a year ... er ... all well and good. Christmas? Let's make it 25 December, because that's the Roman Feast of Saturnalia. Easter? The first Sunday after the full moon following the vernal equinox (March 21 or thereabouts). Add in the fact that the full moon doesn't necessarily have to be full and the other fact that Easter eggs are in the shops on Boxing Day and a dog's breakfast is the only possible outcome.

Someone should really have said to His Holiness back in 1582, 'Chill out, you've got a
Counter-Reformation to sort out. Prioritize, Greg!'
But at least teachers – always known for some reason in this context as 'bloody teachers' – get a few weeks holiday, so don't let's knock it.

Feb 25

The French Impressionist painter Pierre-Auguste Renoir was born today in 1841. He is quoted as saying, 'I never think I have finished a nude until I think I could pinch it.' Other people of course have been trying to pinch Renoirs for years.

In other news ... 432 years ago today Pope Pius V got his chasuble in a twist and excommunicated Elizabeth I. Calling her 'the Jezebel of England', he effectively put out a contract on the queen, saying it was perfectly understandable if good Catholics decided to kill her. Can I just remind you, Seven Queue Gee that Pius (the name means holy) was the head of a Christian church that believed in love, charity, forgiveness and generally being nice.

What had Elizabeth done to upset his Munificence? She'd been born out of wedlock – that's a place in Shropshire, Seven Oh Jay – what *are* the Geography Department teaching you these days?

Feb 26

Today in 1791, the Bank of England issued the first ever pound note. It was nearly four feet square and didn't fold up very well into anybody's purse or wallet. So, two centuries later, they came up with a £1 coin instead. A number of points to consider here before we put our proposals to the IMF.

- Paper money was so new in the 1790s that use of it led to a run on the banks. Imagine – bankers being beaten up in the streets; oh, the joy of it!
- The 'gold' coin that replaced it was briefly called a Thatcher, because it was 'bold, brassy and thinks it's a sovereign'.
- The £1 coin was too small for anybody to write on it 'I promise to pay the bearer the sum of £1' or to carry the all-important signature of the Governor of the Bank of England.
- The current economic crisis has now been going on for so long that 48 per cent (that's over half) of Eight Zed Pee have never seen a £1 coin, although they tell each other stories when they gather round the family dog for warmth of an evening about that great Eldorado that used to exist down the back of the sofa, long since mined out and used to buy essentials like a warmer dog and stamps to go on the begging letters.

Golden days.

> Since the above was written, we now have see-through plastic money, which probably saves trees but adds unnecessarily to the amount of plastic money in the world.

In other news ... Fats Domino was born today in 1928. What were Mr and Mrs Domino thinking, calling their enormously talented little boy Fats? That would be child abuse today, which is why I find it so odd that people who call their kids Bucket, Playstation and Chunnel get away with it.

Feb 27

Henry Wadsworth, he Longfellow,
Born this day in Eighteen Seven,
Wrote a poem, mighty catchy,
Even if the rhymes were patchy
Wrote it longhand, this Longfellow
Because they had yet to invent a personal computer.

In other news ... On this day in 1933, a serious fire gutted the Reichstag, Berlin's parliament building. 'God grant,' said the new chancellor, Adolf Hitler, 'that this is the work of the Communists.' (actually, it was the work of the Nazis). 'You [a foreign correspondent to whom he was to speak] are witnessing the beginning of a great new epoch in German history. This fire is the beginning.'

It was – the Nazis followed up by burning books, then people.

Feb 28

On this day in 1874, Arthur Orton was found guilty of perjury in a trial that had lasted for 260 days (the longest in legal history after that of Warren Hastings, Governor General of India). Orton swore he was the rightful claimant to a small fortune belonging to the Tichborne family and that he was himself Roger Tichborne, the missing heir. The only problem was that Roger was eight stone wringing wet and Arthur had a far more realistic claim to be the fattest man in England.

Don't tell me they were all playing the anti-plump card as early as 1874!

In other news ... Today in 1973 members of the Lakota nation

- that's Sioux if you, like me, were brought up on Western B movies – occupied the village of Wounded Knee in South Dakota in a gesture against the continuing bad treatment of Native Americans – that's Indians if you're a Western fan or Christopher Columbus. In the original 'battle' of Wounded Knee in 1890, the 7th Cavalry, still smarting over the thrashing they got on the Big Horn fourteen years earlier, opened their Gatling guns on unarmed men, women and children led by their chief Big Foot. This was described in the American press as a battle; the defeat of an arrogant idiot called George Custer was described as a massacre,

Go, as modern Americans say, figure.

Feb 29

Make the most of this one – any History that happens today won't happen again for another four years (except the repeats on the Discovery and History channels). As Disraeli once described the 1867 Reform Act, it was 'a leap year in the dark' (don't worry – nobody knew what he was talking about at the time, either).

So, on this day in 1960, Hugh Hefner opened the Playboy Club in Chicago and introduced the world to gorgeous, scantily clad waitresses posing as rabbits. Strictly no hanky-panky however – you can look, but you can't touch. Hefner was brought up a strict Methodist and started his career on a shoestring with *Playboy* magazine (about as racy as *Hello* is today, but mind-bogglingly naughty in its day). So could we say that Hughie is a porn-again Christian? No.

In other news ... A birthday back in 1792 on this day has prompted an idea for a brilliant TV show. Gioacchino Rossini, composer and chef, was born on 29 February (so, of course, he was four on his first birthday – see Gilbert and Sullivan's *Pirates of Penzance* for a mathematical explanation). One of the excellent pieces Rossini composed was the *William Tell Overture*, you know, the one the Lone Ranger used to gallop to on Saturday evening tv back in the '50s – duddle dum, duddle dum, duddle dum dum dum – you know the one. For my younger follower, it is the Dove for Men advert.

Well, combining Rossini's talents, how about a cookery programme (now, there's a novelty) in which a series of terrified, gormless hopefuls have to rustle up, say, Tournedos Rossini at the speed of the Overture? That way, all cookery programmes would last only a few minutes and we could watch something worthwhile.

The programme could be called *The Great Italian Rip-off.*

MARCH

Mar 1

Dewi Sant – St David – what a guy. Patron Saint of Wales. He died in 601 according to the *Annales Cambriae* (that's *Welsh Chronicles* to you, Nine Oh Dee) but that wasn't written until the tenth century, so you can't be sure. He was the Bishop of Moni Judeorum (later St David's) in Pembrokeshire and presided over two Welsh synods (church bashes) ...

... Is that it? You don't have to do much to be a patron saint these days, do you?

In other news ... One of the most over-rated books of all time hit French newsstands today in 1555. It was called the *Book of Centuries* and was written by Michel de Notre Dame, better known by his Latin monicker Nostradamus. In this mischievous piece of nonsense, believed in implicitly by millions worldwide, is a series of predictions including the Great Fire of London (inevitable in a city built on too small an area and almost entirely of wood); the French Revolution (they'd already had several by Nostradamus' time); the rise of Hitler (from a country that had already produced Attila the Hun). In short, nothing surprising at all. As somebody once said, isn't it strange, if Nostradamus was such a know-all, that he didn't see fit to warn us about Pot Noodles?

And there's something even spookier. Did you notice the book was published in 1555? That's not only nearly the Number of the Beast, it's also, according to TV cop shows, the telephone number of everybody in America.

Coo.

But seriously, if you, my sensible follower, know anyone worried by Nostradamus, Mother Shipton, Mayan prophecies and the rest – steer them to *Good Omens* by Gaiman and Pratchett, for a hilarious alternative look at prophecy and the end of days. Even if they are still worried when they have read it, they will at least have had a laugh.

Mar 2

John Wesley died today in 1791. One of a huge family from Epworth in Lincolnshire (the family home is a museum today) Wesley went to Oxford and joined the Holy Club, a group of practical do-gooders at a time when the Church of England, which he also joined, was more concerned with lining its own pockets and only worked one day a week. He brought religion to the people at a time when the dear old C of E had largely abandoned them, preaching in the open air in industrial areas. He was autocratic (his enemies called him Pope John) and his medical remedies could kill you, but if you want a moment of pure peace, visit the Methodist chapel in Bristol where he used to preach. The stable for his horse is just next door and amongst the noise and bustle of a modern city, you are transported back to another time.

Way to go, John.

In other news ... I'm probably a Philistine, but what is it about ballet? The first one to be staged in England, *The Loves of Mars and Venus*, was performed at a Drury Lane theatre on this day back in 1717. Take a dramatic event – let's say the slave revolt of the gladiator Spartacus – and let's have a load of blokes with no strides on (that's a direct quote from Paul Hogan, by the way) jumping around to music.

Spartacus must be turning in his grave. And don't get me started on Billy Elliott!

Mar 3

I'm writing this one in a whisper so that I don't upset the cat. You see, on this day in 1848, his namesake, Count Metternich, was overthrown by rebels in Vienna during the Year of Revolutions. All Hell was let loose all over Europe in fact by people demanding the vote, more food, the setting up of republics, more food, the end of aristocracy and the power of the church and more food. Louis Philippe's palace was destroyed the previous month in France. Venice broke away from Austrian control. There were barricades and burnings and running battles in just about every European capital.

Except London. To be fair, we did have a Chartist rally

(the Chartists were those lunatics who wanted the vote and five other ludicrous demands) but it was typically British. The petition of 5 million names demanding reform actually contained less than 2 million and they included the Duke of Wellington (who would have put himself through the shredder before allowing any kind of reform) and Victoria Rex (King Victoria). Others were Pug Nose, Big Ears etc. All of which goes to show how seriously we British took our politics. Incidentally, in this rally, there were far more policemen than protesters (David Cameron, – **now known as Boris Johnson, of course** * – are you listening?)

*Heady days, when prime ministers lasted longer than a Tunnock's Teacake. It is now, of course (or at least at time of typing), Keir Starmer but that is via Liz Truss and Rishi Sunak. That is four PMs in less than two years, as opposed to the usual maximum of one every five.**

In other news ... Jean Harlow, the platinum blonde star of the new talkie screen was born today in 1911. Margot Asquith, when addressed by the star as Margotte, replied, 'the "t" is silent, as in Harlot [pronouncing it Harlow, of course].' But as Temperance Brennan of *Bones* would say, there is no 't' in Harlow, so that is not only illogical, but it is nonconsequential and ultimately unamusing. Although we at Maxwell Towers have been known to double up over it. It is one up on the 'pee is silent as in the bath' joke – but not by much.

Mar 4

On this day back in 1681 Charles II lost it completely. He signed a treaty giving a huge chunk of territory (which didn't belong to him anyway) to a Quaker called William Penn. Not only that but the king wrote off Penn's debts of £16,000 (£29 million today) and effectively gave Penn the power of a dictator. So grateful was the Quaker that he refused to take his hat off in the royal presence, gave the territory the self-effacing name of Pennsylvania (that's Penn's Wood in case you were wondering, Nine Eff Are) and went on to make a famous breakfast cereal from the oats he used to feed his horse.

Detective Inspector Carpenter-Maxwell and I are applying to Her Majesty this very day to get her to cover our mortgage and outgoings and give us Ottawa or failing that New South Wales. If William Penn can do it ...

In other news ... Saladin died in Damascus today in 1193. His real name was Salah-ed-Din and he was either a nationalist hero or an Arab fundamentalist, depending on your point of view. I go with the first version and there are two stories about him which show what a thorough-going twelfth century gent he was. When Richard the Lionheart (psychopath, homosexual – but that's another story) lay seriously ill with fever during the Third Crusade, Saladin sent him snow from the mountains to bring his temperature down. On another occasion, Richard proved he'd recovered by smashing an anvil in half with his broadsword (see – I told you he was a psychopath) while Saladin threw a silk handkerchief in the air and caught it on the blade of his scimitar which slit the handkerchief in half. How stylish is that?

Neither of these stories is true, of course, but wouldn't it be nice if they were?

Mar 5

The most brilliant fighter plane of all time, the Spitfire, soared over the skies of Britain today in 1936. Built by Vickers with a Rolls Royce Merlin engine, the plane was to prove more than a match for the Messerschmidt 109 which Willi of the same name had already brought out in Germany. I remember seeing an advert (which was never shown for fear of upsetting our dearest partners in the EU – how soon they forget) showing a Spitfire doing a victory roll over the White Cliffs of Dover and the voiceover saying 'Because he was there, we don't have to say "Vorsprung durch technik".'

Thank you, R.J. Mitchell and all the men (and women) who flew them.

In other news ... Eighty-two years ago, Clarence Birdseye came out with his frozen peas. They were round and green and tasted just like the real thing, only colder. Clarence was a New York food scientist and joined the ranks of other cryo-culinarists such as Alvin Findus and Mervyn McCain to bring us such delights as the twenty second sausage and the five second baked potato. To steal a thought from Homer Simpson, reading the back of a ready meal – five seconds! How can anybody wait that long?

Mar 6

My favourite swordsman of all time was born today in 1619. He was Hercule-Savinien Cyrano de Bergerac, novelist, playwright, poet, scientist and owner of the largest nose in showbiz. He is said to have fought over 1000 duels over insults to his hooter and won them all. As a very young teacher I once played him in a school production and judging by Nolan's prowess with a (mercifully plastic!) blade, he might yet follow in his dad's footsteps in the same role.

If you haven't seen the Jose Ferrer film about the guy, made back in the Fifties, make sure you do. If you haven't seen the Gerard Depardieu remake – keep it that way!

> **Recently, James MacAvoy played him *without a large nose* which should rule out about two thirds of the dialogue. It's a bit like Quasimodo being a fit bloke off of Love Island.**

In other news ... Oscar Strauss was born on this day in 1870. His birthplace was Vienna and he wrote the opera *The Chocolate Soldier.* But he was totally eclipsed by his Jewish cousin, Levi, who invented jeans. Both men suffered from Post Traumatic Strauss Disorder.

Mar 7

Today is International Rhine Crossing day and several thousand will be doing it, the Germans going one way and Everybody Else the other. The first crossing took place on this day in 1936 when Nazi troops moved into the Demilitarized Zone that had been set up by the Treaty of Versailles in 1919. Prime Minister

Stanley Baldwin told Herr Hitler not to do it again, but the Fuhrer couldn't speak English, so it was rather a waste of time.

Exactly nine years later, American troops crossed the river at Remagen with the express intention of shouting a bit louder at the Fuhrer, this time in German so he could understand it.

In other news ... Today was the day when the enlightened Swiss, originators of yodelling, cheese and national heroes who are whizzo shots with a crossbow gave women the vote. The day was 7 March but what was the year, I hear you cry? 1748? 1812? No, it was 1971, making Swiss men about as enlightened and democratic as Attila the Hun.

Mar 8

The Blind Beggar shooting, took place today, back in 1966. The bullet holes are still there in the wall of the pub, down Whitechapel way, a well-known venue of drinkers who were blind (hence the name), deaf, or mates of the Kray brothers (damn, I've given it away!)

In other news ... Script writers of American soaps like *Dynasty* and *Dallas* went on strike today in 1988. There were fears that both series could come to an end, but, sadly, the dispute was resolved.

The result? Binge-watching and Netflix.

Mar 9

William Cobbett was born today in 1763. If you've never heard of this guy, shame on you. He wrote a book called *Rural Rides* in 1824 which was one long whinge against anything new. If you remember Richard Wilson in *One Foot In The Grave* or you are addicted to *Grumpy Old Men*, Cobbett's the boy for you. He hated paper money (usually because he didn't have any); the government (although he tried to be part of it); standing armies (even though he was once a soldier); and London (despite the fact that he lived there). He was his own worst enemy and constantly contradicted himself. In one of his brilliant pamphlets he says what brilliant, friendly, freedom loving people the Americans are and in another he says every American town should be burned to the ground.

William Cobbett, King of the U Turn.

In other news ... The French Foreign Legion was founded today back in 1831. It was a tough outfit, only taking real men like Gary Cooper and Brian Donlevy. Its unofficial motto was March or Die, although more often than not, that meant March *and* Die, but at least you were in good old-fashioned black-n-white company.

Mar 10

On this day in 1974 a Japanese soldier on the island of Lubang in the Philippines finally surrendered. Everybody else had given up on the Second World War after the Enola Gay and Co dropped their bombloads on Nagasaki and Hiroshima, but clearly the news hadn't reached Lubang.

God knows how traumatised this latter day Ben Gunn must have been or how he survived, but his back pay on his war pension must have been stonking!

In other news ... Ninety-eight years ago, Ms Mary Richardson went berserk in the National Gallery. Was it the cost of the delicacies in the tea rooms? The fumes given off by so much gouache and oils? No, Ms Richardson was a Suffragette and was suddenly incensed by the sight of Velasquez' *Rokeby Venus*. She attacked it with a meat cleaver. No doubt she would claim she did so because *that* sort of painting degrades women, but it seems a particularly dastardly attack because neither the Venus nor Velasquez could fight back.

I personally believe that Ms Richardson was furious because the Venus had a nicer bum than she did. But it's not my place to say so.

Mar 11

Herman Goering (fat bloke, liked flashy uniforms, friend of Hitler's) said some pretty stupid things in his time but top of the list must be his comment on this day in 1935. Setting up the brand-new Luftwaffe (which, by the way, broke the terms of the Treaty of Versailles – again!) he said, 'The Americans cannot build aeroplanes. They are very good at refrigerators and razor blades.'

I wonder if he remembered those words when American Flying Fortresses were passing over Berlin and flattening the buildings of Goering's Third Reich? By the time the war was actually over, and Germans were avidly buying American fridges and razor blades, Herman the German was dead.

In other news ... On this day in 1702, England's first daily newspaper, confined to London, appeared. It was called the *Daily Courant* and had photos of Queen Anne going walkabout among her subjects. A dream cottage was on offer (subject to terms and conditions) and the editorial carried a bold article on how many illegal Walloons had snuck past emigration authorities. In sporting news, there was a blank page because nobody had invented Rugby yet, football was a game played by oafs (no change there, then) and cricketers used a curved bat so that didn't count.

The girl on Page 3 wore more clothes than the average bag lady, which brings us neatly back to Queen Anne.

The editor – of course – was Master Rupert Murdoch.

Mar 12

When I was a young shaver a couple of Americans wrote and performed a song called *Mrs Robinson*. This was voted record of the year today in 1969 and we all went to see the unknown Dustin Hoffman in *The Graduate* where it appeared again. So did Mrs Robinson, played by the deliciously naughty Anne Bancroft.

So thanks, guys, to Messrs Simon and Garfunkel, Hoffman and Bancroft for making a young man very happy.

'Here's to you, Mrs Robinson!'

In other news ... The British army occupied Bordeaux today in 1813 under the command of Arthur Wellesley, the Viscount Wellington (he got the Dukedom later). This was the memorable occasion when he said of his sweating, grunting infantry, 'I don't know what effect these men will have on the enemy, but by God, they frighten me.'

They frightened the French too and I'm afraid I don't have room today for a list of all their victories.

Ah, the Entente Uncordiale!

Mar 13

The French claimed the first ever professional striptease act took place on this day in the Davan Fourneau Music Hall in Paris in 1894. Alas the Hebrews beat them to it by nearly 2,000 years because Salome was constantly taking her clothes off at the time of Christ. To be fair, though, if we accept the definition of professional as getting paid for it, Salome was the stepdaughter of a king and didn't need the money. Instead, she settled for payment in kind – 'Bring me the head of the Davan Fourneau Music Hall in Paris,' she cried.

In other news ... Russian revolutionaries blew off the legs of Tsar Alexander II today in 1881. The first bomb missed his carriage as he travelled the streets of St Petersburg but the second was thrown as he stopped to ask after the injured. As a result, his son postponed implementing any of Russia's much-needed reforms indefinitely, even though Alexander had already freed the serfs and was promising to implement democracy.

So, who caused the Russian Revolution of 1917? The Narodnya extremists back in 1881.

Mar 14

Karl Marx died on this day in London in 1883. His friend and co-writer Friedrich Engels described him as the 'best-hated man of his time' and that was *before* the Americans had ever heard of him. His book, *The Communist Manifesto*, written in

German in London in 1848 is *very* short, *very* repetitive and has one good line – 'You have nothing to lose but your chains'. As a blueprint for revolution (as tried out by Lenin, Trotsky etc) it doesn't work. As an appeal to human nature it fails too. As for Marx himself, he spent most of his later life scrounging off Engels and has a truly awful tombstone in London's otherwise fantastic Highgate Cemetery.

Marx out of 10? 1.5

In other news ... On this day 48 years ago, dodgy nightclub owner Jack Ruby was found guilty of murdering Lee Harvey Oswald, the presumed assassin of JFK in Dealey Plaza, Dallas five months earlier. If Ruby wasn't part of a conspiracy himself then his removal of Oswald goes beyond the criminal. Had Oswald stood trial we might all know what happened that day in Dallas and a whole JFK industry would never have been born.

Ruby's motive in shooting Oswald at point blank range in front of TV cameras when Oswald was in police custody was 'I did it for Jackie Kennedy'.

Yeah, right.

Mar 15

A few days ago, I popped in to our local soothsayer, who warned me to watch my back today, it being the Ides of March.

Hang on ... Somebody at the door ....

Apparently, it's Casca, just wants a word. I'll be back shortly ...

Mar 16

On this day way back in 1792, Tipu Sahib surrendered to the British. He was Sultan of Mysore in southern India and had all his guns made in Britain (as you do when you're fighting against the most industrialised nation on earth). He was defeated by General Cornwallis who had surrendered to the Americans at Yorktown a few years earlier (nice to know he could win something). Check out (as Cornwallis's victors say) the mechanical toy called Tipu's Tiger. It's a metal lifesize tiger clawing a white man to death and before somebody lost the key it could move its front paws and growl.

Awesome.

In other news ... Two hundred and ten years ago a military college for gentlemen was founded at West Point along the Hudson River. It's gratifying to know that cadets still wear the grey tail-coat and shako of the 1820s and that West Point produced some of America's worst soldiers (Custer) and best (... erm ...).

Mar 17

Gottleib Daimler was born today in 1834. He was one of the many pioneers of the motor car and aren't we all grateful that cars were named after their inventors' surnames rather than Christian names, otherwise we'd have had, along with the fabulous Gottleibs, Henrys, Charleses, Karls, Andre-Gustaves and Edsels ... oh, wait a minute, there really *was* an Edsel.

You take my point.

In other news ... It's one of those irritating pub quiz questions; who invented the elastic band? The answer is Stephen Perry, who was born today in 1845. One wonders why he did it. I'd like to think it was to twang bits of screwed up paper around a classroom to annoy his teachers, but it couldn't have been because, looking at his dates, one of them would have (quite rightly) beaten him to death.

Mar 18

An Austrian army defeated a French Revolutionary one at Neerminden today in 1793. This was the last time Austria won anything, except possibly a Eurovision Song Contest.

In other news ... The first telephone line was set up between London and Paris today in 1891. The conversation (which was recorded for training purposes) went like this:

- Hello?
- Allo?
- Hello? Can you hear me?
- Allo?
- Can ... you ... hear ... me?
- Allo?
- CAN ... YOU ... HEAR ... ME?

Merde!

Mar 19

The Tolpuddle Martyrs went down today in 1834. George and James Loveless and five of their farm labourer mates were sentenced to seven years' transportation to Botany Bay in Australia. Their crime? They joined a branch of the Grand National Consolidated Trade Union in an attempt to improve the pitiful wages paid to labourers. Local Dorset farmers connived with the county's magistrates to find a way to punish the men because, technically, joining a Trade Union was not illegal.

They came up with administering (taking) of illegal oaths, which was a crime under the 1797 Mutiny Act. According to the law at the time, the Martyrs had no opportunity to defend themselves in court and could not afford a lawyer. One of them died in Australia before public outrage brought the survivors back. It would be forty years before anybody tried to set up another union for farm workers and the conspiracy of landowners and magistrates would continue for much longer.

In other news ... Edgar Rice Burroughs, the creator of Tarzan of the Apes, died today in 1950.
His 70 novels had been translated into 56 languages and more than 100 million copies had been sold. On his gravestone they wrote Tarzan's immortal words –

'AAAAAAAAAARRGHHYYAAAAAA!'

Who could ask for a finer epitaph?

Mar 20

One of the most influential books of all time went on sale today in 1852. It was Harriet Beecher Stowe's *Uncle Tom's Cabin* which was a tear-jerker set in a slave plantation in the Deep South. Queen Victoria read it and wept buckets. There is no doubt that the book, very widely read in the United States, had a powerful effect on the tensions already running high in America. Mrs Beecher Stowe had never seen a plantation in her life, so we have to raise questions about the book's accuracy. President Lincoln summed it up best with his famous words when he met her. 'So you're the little woman who started this great war of ours.'

Didn't mince words, did Honest Abe.

In other news ... Another American book hit the headlines today in 1841. It was Edgar Allen Poe's *The Murder in the Rue Morgue*, one of the first detective stories that launched a genre. Poe himself was an odd character, obsessed with the macabre and died a hopeless alcoholic in a Baltimore street wearing somebody else's clothes (but that's another story).

The *Rue Morgue* is a great page turner, but today, no doubt, some of the mystery would have been removed by the inevitable subtitle spoiler - The Murders in the Death Street; the Monkey Did It.

(Apologies to any of you who didn't know the monkey did it ... rather like the policeman in the *Mousetrap* it is fairly obvious once you know.)

(Apologies to any of you who didn't know the policeman did it ...)

Mar 21

The Lord Chief Justice, Herbert Parker, gave the world a fascinating insight into the psyche of judges today in 1961. He said, 'A judge is not supposed to know anything about the facts of life until they have been presented in evidence and explained to him at least three times.'

This was also the time when another judge asked the jury in his summing up in the obscenity case concerning D.H. Lawrence's *Lady Chatterley's Lover* whether this was a book you would allow your servants to read. Both judges were practising when the death penalty still operated in Britain.

Scary, isn't it?

In other news ... On this day in 1908, the aviator Henri Farman flew over Paris with the first ever air passenger on board his aircraft. There is no truth in the rumour that the man was bound and gagged or that he was suicidal.

He was just high as a kite.

Mar 22

Anthony van Dyck was born today in 1599. Famous for his court portraits of Charles I. He later went on the star in his father's long-running TV series *Diagnosis Murder*.

In other news ... Today in 1906 the first international rugby match took place with England beating France 35-0. The England team had already scored pretty heavily at Crecy, Poitiers, Agincourt, Ramillies, Malplaquet, Sahagun, Badajoz, Toulouse and Waterloo. An earlier result at Hastings, where the French unaccountably won, was deemed to be because they played with the roof open.

Mar 23

On this day in 1925, the state of Tennessee decided that the theory of evolution should not be taught in schools because it was contrary to scriptures. All the other subjects were also banned because there was no specific reference to them in the Bible. Except Maths (oops, sorry, Math) because of the Book of Numbers.

In other news ... Pedro the Cruel of Castile and Leon was murdered on this day in 1369 on the orders of his brother Henry, the Even More Cruel. Their mother, Isabella the Outraged, was appalled (told you she would be) especially since she had hoped the crown would pass to her youngest son, Rodrigo the Utterly Unprincipled.

In more personal news, DI Mrs Carpenter-Maxwell would like to thank her many wellwishers and she is happy to announce the impending happy event of her plaster removal, next Monday, all being well and taking into account following winds, hordes of magpies, not walking under ladders and other arcane behaviour. Speaking personally, I won't miss the demise of half a ton of cast which has reliably called me into wakefulness several times a night by clouting me round the head for the last five weeks. Nolan is looking forward to a two-armed cuddle. Metternich is the only one who will lose out – his Mistress's enforced rest-time while Mrs Troubridge and I have been busy with the housekeeping has given him lap opportunities hitherto only dreamed of.

Mar 24

Queen Elizabeth I (Gloriana to her friends) died today in 1603 ushering out the Tudors and ushering in the Stuarts. Her last words were 'All my possessions for a moment of time'. Which got me thinking about last words generally. There was Prime Minister William Pitt's 'I could just eat one of Mrs Bellamy's meat pies'. There was General Robert E Lee's 'Strike the tents!'

And we mustn't forget Harold Godwinson's famous line at Hastings just before the arrow got him – 'Things are definitely looking up.' Some people of course claim that his last words were 'Watch that bloke with the bow and arrow – he could have somebody's eye out' – but that would be plain silly.

In other news ... Field Marshal Bernard Montgomery hung up his baton today in 1976. He was an arrogant so-and-so who for reasons best known to himself wore an RAF flying jacket and a beret with *two* badges. If that doesn't scream schizophrenia, I don't know what does. Every member of his 8th Army I've ever met, not excepting my dear old dad, hated him.

But he won battles.

Mar 25

Parliament abolished the slave trade on this day in 1807. The prime mover here was William Wilberforce who had been banging his head against an uncaring system for years. It would be another quarter of a century before the *owning* of slaves was abolished and then, the former owners were paid a fortune in compensation.

(For any Year Tens reading this, thank a teacher ... sorry, wrong slogan. I mean, should you be worrying about that essay on slavery now scarily near its deadline, there are several excellent films you can watch and pretend to your parents you are working. One is the splendid *Amistad*, the other *Amazing Grace*. *Twelve Years a Slave* is decidedly iffy by comparison).

A pity the Americans didn't follow suit however. Hanging on to the 'peculiar institution' of slavery until 1863 cost them a civil war which was the bloodiest in American history.

Next time, dudes, take a leaf out of our book.

In other news ... You've probably seen the excellent film *The Last King of Scotland* in which the late and unlamented Ugandan dictator Idi Amin strides around in a kilt and glengarry. Because of what happened today in 1306 somebody should start shooting another epic called *The First Australian King of Scotland*.

Why?

Because today in 1306 the eighth earl of Carrick took the Scots throne. His name was Robert the Bruce.

Mar 26

Today in 1923 the great Sarah Bernhardt took her exit. having her leg amputated as a result of a fall in *Tosca*, she had a wooden one fitted and continued to act all sorts of roles, male and female. she appeared on more Art Nouveau posters than you've had hot dinners and slept in a coffin.

They don't make them like her any more.

In other news ... Leonard Nimoy was born today in 1931. Yes, he was often the baddie in various TV westerns but rose to fame as Mr Spock, the Vulcan baby expert in *Star Trek*. It must have been very difficult to hide those pointy ears before this role called for it; hence, I suppose, the westerns. A stetson covers little deformities like that.

May he live long and prosper.

Mar 27

Today in 1964 a gang of old lags who had robbed a train were sentenced to 307 years imprisonment. Known as the Great Train Robbers, although neither they nor the train were particularly great, they'll be out, with good behaviour in 2264. And the £2.6 million they stole will be worth £47.16.

As my good lady wife constantly reminds me, crime doesn't pay.

In other news ... A great tragedy took place today in 1968 and a great irony too. Yuri Gagarin was the first astronaut to orbit the earth in a brilliant achievement that won the admiration of the world. But he died in a car crash near Moscow. It's probably safer in Space.

Or Slough, as it turns out – figures out today quote Slough as the safest place to drive. The town has recently decommissioned its speed cameras. Hmmmm ....

As White Surrey's top speed has never bothered a speed camera I am not really qualified to comment on things motoring, but I think 'I told you so' fits the bill!

Mar 28

One of the biggest b*****s in British history died today in 1868. He was James Brudenell, the 7th Earl of Cardigan and he is famous for leading the Charge of the Light Brigade down the wrong valley at Balaclava during the Crimean War. He was arrogant, impetuous and deeply stupid, buying his way through the cavalry ranks with his enormous private income. His men quite liked him; to them he was Jim the Bear because he growled a lot. His officers detested him however and he made their lives hell just because he could. He should never have been given a regiment to command, still less a cavalry brigade.

Ironically, he died from a fall from his horse.

In other news ... The British Navy sank seven Italian warships on this day in 1941 at the battle of Matapan, off Crete. The British suffered no losses and the battle is commemorated every year during the Six Nations Rugby competition when there is always a similar scoreline between Fortress Twickenham and the Azzurri.

Mar 29

Back in 1886, Dr John Pemberton came out with a corker. It was March 29 and he thought the world – or at least Allanton, Georgia – was ready for a drink that could cure hysteria, the common cold and just about everything in between. It was an 'Esteemed Brain Tonic' (for esteemed brains only) and an 'Intellectual Beverage' (which is why the Mem and I drink it and Eight Eff Pee never touch the stuff). It was made from caffeine, syrup and Coca leaves. It was called – you guessed it – Syrup of Figs.

Lovely.

In other news ... This one must float to the top in the What-Was-That-All-About stakes. Today in 1989, to commemorate two hundred years of mass guillotinings, President Francois Mitterand unveiled a glass 'thing' in front of the Louvre. Astonishingly, bearing in mind the scorn the pyramid drew, it's not only still there but actually featured in the movie *The Da Vinci Code*.

You couldn't make it up, could you? That's because Dan Brown did.

I know editors ought to keep their traps shut unless totally necessary, but nevertheless, I am barging in here to wish a happy birthday to Richard, publisher extraordinare!

Mar 30

One of the screen's great hero baddies died today in 1986. He was a song and dance man straight out of Vaudeville but made his name in gangster movies with a wise-cracking style and a line everybody can do – 'You dirty rat!' If you want to see the late, great James Cagney at his best, watch his *Shake Hands With the Devil* in which he plays a deranged IRA member and *Angels With Dirty Faces* – that walk to the electric chair can't fail to bring tears to your eyes.

In other news ... The Spanish artist Francisco Goya was born today in 1746. He's the guy who painted Arthur Wellesley, Duke of Wellington, who used to appear on English money before they started using various ever-more-obscure people who had something-or-other to do with the Industrial Revolution. Goya's sketches of Wellington's war in Spain are horrific, with arms and legs hanging in trees. He painted a pretty spooky witch or two as well.

Even the Head of Art at Leighford High has heard of him, so he must be famous!

Mar 31

On this day in 1905, Dr Arthur Conan Doyle had to resurrect his brilliant detective hero, Sherlock Holmes. Everybody thought the world's greatest detective had gone over the Reichenbach Falls with Dr Moriarty, arch villain and the 'Napoleon of Crime'. Sadly, no. The good doctor claimed an adoring public demanded Holmes' return, but I think he had a tax bill due.

In other news ...
Richard Chamberlain was born on this day in 1935. I remember watching Dr Kildare as a kid and was fascinated by the actor's

ability to stop dead in the middle of whatever he was doing. This was a long time before they invented the freeze-frame technology, so, good on you, Richard. You were ahead of your time.

APRIL

April 1

Now, I know what you're thinking ... how can we trust anything he writes today? And you'd be right!

See you all tomorrow!

April 2

You know how things get misreported in history? There was a classic today in 1802 when Horatio Nelson, he of the column, turned a blind eye to orders and sank the Danish fleet in Copenhagen harbour. His ship, the *Elephant,* was under heavy fire and he received an order from the commander in chief, Sir Hyde Parker (brother of Sir Regent's Parker) to pull out. Most people will tell you that Nelson put his telescope to his glass eye and said, 'I see no ships,' which is pretty ludicrous bearing in mind he was shooting at them. He didn't even say, 'I see no signal,' because somebody asked him if he saw the signal from Parker's ship (done by flags) and he replied, 'Damn me if I do.' Now that sounds more like Hor and very much in keeping with the Duke of Wellington's coming out confession of fourteen years later – 'Napoleon has humbugged me, by God.'

And yes, follower, I know that Nelson didn't have a glass eye, despite whole museum exhibits devoted to them!

In other news ... The first Italian parliament met on this day in 1860 in Turin, which was odd, because the parliament building was in Rome. That pretty much set the seal on Italian politics from that moment on.

April 3

Jesse James got his today in 1882. Known as 'Dingus' as a kid, he was one of the first psychopaths in history to blame his upbringing – in his case the Civil War. He and his brother Frank took to robbing trains after a killing spree with Quantrill's Raiders and he tried to go straight later, happily married with two kids and calling himself Thomas Howard. There was however a $10,000 reward out for him and that was claimed by Bob Ford who shot him in the back of the head while Jesse was standing on a chair straightening a picture on the wall. The result was *The Assassination of Jesse James*, probably the most boring film ever made. And as everyone knows, for me to find a Western boring, it has to be extremely boring indeed.

In other news ... One of the greatest miscarriages of justice took place today in 1936 when Bruno Hauptmann went to the electric chair for the kidnapping of the baby son of Charles Lindbergh, the famous aviator. The police decided that Hauptmann was guilty largely because he was an immigrant and they may have trumped up evidence against him.

Case closed? Don't you believe it!

April 4

Francis Drake became *Sir* Francis Drake today in 1581 when he was knighted by Queen Elizabeth at Deptford on the deck of his ship, the *Pelican*, renamed the *Golden Hind*. He had left Plymouth on 13 December 1577 with 5 ships and a total crew of 160, as well as various sponsors.

He was now able to state conclusively that the world was indeed round as Magellan had already proved and Columbus believed. Presumably, if Drake had been knighted on 1 April, he would have told the queen the earth was flat.

In other news ... Ben Hur won eleven Oscars today in 1960 and rightly so. I was still of very tender years when I saw this one and I loved every minute. There was rugged, gritty Charlton Heston, *every* boy's hero; gorgeous Haya Harareet as the love interest; Stephen Boyd as a thoroughly nasty Messala and of course that superb chariot race which *still* has me on the edge of my seat. It was probably the last film that coyly didn't show the face of Christ – just his lovely red hair from the back. For film trivia buffs and quiz compilers out there, the actor who played him was Claude Heater and wasn't even in the credits. Sheik Ilderim was played by Welshman Hugh Griffith and the wise man Balthazar by a Scotsman, Findlay Currie, but they were both excellent. Add in the Irish Stephen Boyd and it should come as no surprise to learn that Pontius Pilate (boo! hiss!) was played by an Australian, the onomatopoeic Frank Thring.

The only other film to do as well in Oscar terms was *Titanic*. Oh per-lease!

April 5

Three Hollywood legends were born on this day, albeit a few years apart. Spencer Tracy was the first, in 1900, who lent his gravitas to a brilliant version of *Jekyll and Hyde* and *Northwest Passage*. He could also play a hard man – *Bad Day at Black Rock* – as well as high comedy – *It's a Mad, Mad, Mad, Mad World*. Movie Trivia – Tracy's first job on screen was as a nonspeaking robot, alongside his lifelong friend, Pat O'Brien.

Bette Davis followed in 1908, playing femmes fatales from *The Letter* to *Whatever Happened to Baby Jane*. Movie Trivia – she was famously taken off by Liz Taylor in *Who's Afraid of Virginia Woolf?* – 'What a dump!'

Last comes the baby of the bunch, dear old Gregory Peck, he of the raised eyebrow. He was outstanding as Atticus Finch in *To Kill a Mockingbird* and I liked him (but nobody else did) as Captain Ahab in *Moby Dick*. But then I am one of the few people living who has read the book – although I had to have a good long lie down afterwards.

Movie Trivia – Atticus Finch was voted the greatest screen hero of all time in 2003, beating Indiana Jones and James Bond into 2nd and 3rd places respectively – and quite right too!

In other news ... Poor old Oscar Wilde went on trial today in 1895. He brought his misfortunes on himself by bringing libel charges against the appalling Marquess of Queensbury, whose son Alfred ('Bosie') was one of Wilde's lovers. The whole thing backfired disastrously and Wilde, previously the darling of the West End theatre-going public, ended up in Reading Gaol with two years' hard labour.

The love that dare not speak its name was criminalized by Henry Labouchere MP in his Criminal Law Amendment Act of 1884 and was the famous occasion when Queen Victoria used the royal veto because she thought lesbians were the natives of Lesbos!

Aren't our royal family wonderful?

April 6

Richard the Lionheart died today in 1199 as a result of an infected arrow wound to the neck while besieging a castle at Chaluz in France. He is one of those historical characters who has been hi-jacked by the mythmakers, usually turning up at the end of Robin Hood films in time to realize that his nasty brother John has already been well and truly trounced by Robin himself.

The real Richard was only in the country for six months of his ten year reign, was probably homosexual and definitely psychopathic – like most of the Plantagenets.

In other news ... Today in 1814 Napoleon Bonaparte was forced to abdicate after a whirlwind military career which saw him as master of most of Europe. He was to be sent to Elba which was a big mistake as it was only a stone's throw from his old stomping ground (France) *and* he was allowed to retain a largish bodyguard (10,000 men). Surprise, surprise, he escaped and started the whole mayhem all over again.

You can't keep a good dictator down.

April 7

One of the greatest inventors in history was born today in 1891. We've all heard of Thomas Edison, James Watt, James Dyson, Richard Arkwright (well, Twelve Pee Zed, perhaps not Richard Arkwright, more's the pity) but what of the late, great Ole Kirk Christiansen, I hear you ask?

Generations have been grateful to him and he even had a land named after his invention. What did he invent?

Lego.

In other news ... Richard Turpin was hanged in York on this day in 1739. His story is fascinating because the actual psychotic low-life who once roasted an old lady's backside on a red hot grate until she told him where she kept her valuables was turned into a hero by a single novel – Harrison Ainsworth's in the 1830s. Turpin's horse, Black Bess, his legendary ride to York before they built the A1, his derring-do and concern for the poor is all pure fiction.

April 8

The Russian ballet dancer Vaslav Nijinsky died today in 1950. The poor man had taken very early retirement (at 29) because he was suffering from schizophrenia. Half the time he thought he was a racehorse.

In other news ... Jan van Riebeeck of the Dutch East India Company, gave orders to his men landing at the Cape of Good Hope in 1652 that anybody who mistreated an African was to receive fifty lashes of the whip in the presence of their victim.

How ironic that the descendants of these men slaughtered hundreds of Zulus at Blood River in 1836 and went on to set up Apartheid in our own time.

April 9

Isambard Kingdom Brunel was born today in 1806. The greatest engineer of his age, he built the Clifton suspension bridge, the Great Western Railway with its 7ft 1/4 inch gauge and the SS *Great Britain* steamship. The photo of him standing in front of the ship's anchor chains with his top hat on and a cigar clamped firmly in his lips is the epitome of the self-made man. They named a university after him and one or two of My Own Sixth Form have gone on to fine things at the University of Isambard.

In other news ... Francis Bacon died today in Highgate, London in 1626. He was a statesman, philosopher, Attorney-General, probable spy and quite a good egg (I am writing this on Easter

Sunday, so eggs are very much on my mind as well as smeared down one trouser leg and thoroughly coating the cat, thanks to Nolan and his dear little egg-hunting friends from Mrs Whatmough's Academy For Young Delinquents). Rumour has it that he died of a cold brought on by trying to freeze a chicken by stuffing it with snow. If only he'd gone to Tesco's, like the rest of us.

April 10

Bananas were on sale in Britain for the first time today in 1633. They are excellent, professional readers will tell you, for preventing growling or rumbling tummies, *fatal* for sound recordings (the rumbling, that is, not the bananas). An EU directive tried to straighten them out some years ago, but it didn't work because the directive came from Brussels (which are round and green and responsible for much of the rumbling mentioned above).

In other news ... Cairo Fred was born today in 1932. He is better known as Omar Sharif and is one of the world's best backgammon players (as Lord Lucan was, but Mr Sharif didn't murder his children's nanny or done a runner). Remember Omar coming out of that heat haze on a camel in *Lawrence of Arabia*? Magic.

April 11

A remarkable character was born today in 1929. He served in the US Navy, smoked a pipe all his life and had a deformed jaw. He only had one friend, who was addicted to beefburgers and his girlfriend left a lot to be desired in the hourglass figure stakes. He was constantly having run-ins with a moron with a beard and huge shoulders and there was a kid who looked just like him and was always crawling off high buildings. Robin Williams played him – not very well, it must be said. His real claim to fame was trying to get children – or indeed any sane adult – to eat spinach.

Thank you, Popeye, for what you've been.

In other news ... William Anne Mary was crowned today in 1689, the only official hermaphrodite monarch of England (the unofficial ones, if you're wondering are: Richard I, Edward II and [almost] Wallis Simpson).

April 12

President Harry S Truman got it right today in 1958 when he said 'A politician is a man who understands government ... A statesman is a politician who's been dead for ten or fifteen years.'

Spot on, S.

In other news ... This was the day, legend says, when the Union Jack became the official flag of Britain. The only problem is when? Some accounts say 1606, three years after England and Scotland were first ruled by the same king (James VI or I depending on your grasp of Latin, maths and country of origin).

Others say 1707, when the Act of Union formally united England and Scotland. Ireland didn't join (much against its better judgement) until 1801. So who knows? It didn't help of course that the flag only reflects England and Scotland in the crosses of St George and St Andrew, their respective patron saints. St David (Wales) and St Patrick (Ireland) didn't have heraldic crosses and I suspect the English and Scots were pretty miffed that the dragon and the shamrock made much more interesting heraldic designs, so the Union Jack ignores them completely.

April 13

Friday 13th! This is the day that Ten Bee Eff will kick off big time, the entire school IT system crashes and they're only serving semolina in the Dining Hall.

But in the real world ... Today in 1860, Tom Hamilton galloped into Sacramento, California carrying forty-nine letters and three newspapers. He was riding the last leg of the first 1,800-mile delivery service of the Pony Express. Riders carried two extra horses (not literally, of course – that would be just silly) and leapt on and off the saddle with the skill of rodeo stars. The news was spread at twice the speed of the Overland Stage Company. I think our dear old Royal Mail could learn a few things from them.

In other news ... Today in 1882 the Anti-Semitic League was founded in Prussia. This group went on to believe a forged document called the Protocols of Zion which 'proved' attempts at world domination by the Jews and were no doubt overjoyed when Adolf Hitler wrote *Mein Kampf.* The sons of the League became the Nazis of the Thirties and did their best to wipe out the Jewish people, resulting in the estimated 55 million fatalities of the Second World War.

April 14

Abraham and Mrs Lincoln went to the theatre today in 1865. The President sat in a box at Ford's Theatre in Washington, chuckling over *Our American Cousin* when a lunatic called John Wilkes Booth put a Derringer slug in the back of Lincoln's head. He then jumped onto the stage shouting 'Sic Semper Tyranis!' (so it always is with tyrants) before limping off with a broken ankle.

Security around the President was lamentable, as it was in the cases of the three other Presidents who have been assassinated.

The event, however, gave rise to the famous black joke – 'But apart from that, Mrs Lincoln, how did you enjoy the play?'

In other news ... Today in 1931 the Highway Code appeared. It was a long overdue attempt to regulate the free-for-all on Britain's roads and has been replaced recently by a much more accurate one, the first page of which I quote below:

1. Never dip your headlights at night* – that sort of courtesy went out with Gottleib Daimler.
2. If you approach an obstacle on your side of the road,

<u>just drive past it,</u> forcing the vehicle coming in the other direction to brake sharply.

3. <u>If you are over 70 years of age</u> you can travel at six miles an hour even on motorways. Six people over 80 per year are allowed to travel the wrong way up a motorway for a distance of not less than 100 miles. Watch press for vacancies.

4. During the school run, all rules of the road <u>must be ignored</u> and the rear-view mirror is for adjusting makeup and admonishing children only.

5. If you are in charge of an HGV, feel free to straddle the white line and <u>flash your lights</u> at other HGV drivers.

6. If you are in charge of a bicycle, by all means wobble all over the road, especially going uphill because you don't understand the gears. You can of course mount the pavement whenever you like because that silly bit of plastic on your head makes you <u>100% invulnerable.</u>

7. If you are in charge of a horse, make sure you have <u>no control over the animal at all;</u> if possible be under fifteen years old and always ride two abreast on country lanes chatting to your mate. If your mate doesn't have a horse, they can ride their bicycle alongside (see point 6 above).

8. **All motorways are smart and the hard shoulder is something you used to get in rugby matches, now banned by Elf 'n' Safety.**

We've really come on since 1931 haven't we?

*For those who continue to doubt my keyboard skills, please note the use of <u>Underlined.</u> I don't know how I did it, but it certainly looks the business.

April 15

Our boys in blue went on strike today in 1797. No, not the police – they hadn't been set up yet – but the navy, the Jolly Jack

Tars of Old England. It was a bummel of a year all round – the Irish were threatening revolt (what's new?); there was a run on the banks (time for another one, I can't help feeling) and then the fleets at Spithead and the Nore refused to sail against Revolutionary France.

The sailors had an awful lot of legitimate gripes and the way the mutineers were handled says it all. At the Nore, where officers were beaten up, the Admiralty hanged the ringleaders and the fleet sailed, At Spithead, kindly old Admiral Howe invited the ringleaders to his best port and promised them better food and conditions – and the fleet sailed.

Take a lesson, Mr Cameron (**now Johnson, of course**). If the teachers threaten strike action over pay and pensions, give them what they want. If petrol tanker drivers threaten strikes, hang them. That would be fair.

In other news ... Today in 1945, allied troops liberating Europe found a horde of looted Nazi treasure in a mine in Austria. The find included works by Goya, Rubens, da Vinci and Raphael as well as King Arthur's sword Excalibur, King John's Crown Jewels, the Ark of the Covenant and some postcards painted by Adolf Hitler. **All this has been faithfully recreated in an odd and rather sweet little film, *The Monuments Men.***

April 16

I absolutely refuse to mention the Titanic, so ...

In other news ... One of the most lop-sided military encounters in history took place today in 1746. At Culloden Moor, 'Bonnie' Prince Charlie, the Young Pretender, was defeated by an English Army under William, Duke of Cumberland. The Highlanders were outnumbered and outgunned, with no cavalry and virtually no artillery. They were also cold, exhausted and starving before the fight began. As a result of Cumberland's victory the Jacobite threat to the English throne was over and the English named a flower after him – Sweet William. Not to be outdone in the horticultural stakes, the Scots named a weed after him – Stinking Billy.

April 17

A long time ago, when children were literate enough to appreciate corny historical jokes, Messrs Sellar and Yeatman wrote their immortal *1066 And All That*. One of the many gems in the book concerned Martin Luther and his diet of worms. The Diet was actually, for the record, an assembly held in the German town of Worms to decide on the fate of Martin Luther, who appeared on a charge of heresy on this day in 1521.

Today, 83 per cent of children think Martin Luther was a civil rights leader who had a dream and was assassinated in 1968. The other 42 per cent don't think at all.

In other news ... Sir Leonard Woolley, the archaeologist, was born today in 1880. Best known for his excavations at the Persian city of ... um ... Ur, he was the first to find a frozen mammoth and gave his name to it. Several more Leonard mammoths have been found since.

There has been serious progress made on cloning a mammoth from material found in the permafrost. I hope this doesn't really take off, not only because the thought of herds of mammoths sweeping majestically across the landscape of Sussex can only bring problems such as piles of mammoth poo and long tailbacks of traffic caused by one taking its ease on the A23, but on a more personal level, I don't think the cat flap is big enough for when Metternich brings one down in the shrubbery.

April 18

Today in 1955 Albert Einstein died at Princeton hospital. Hailed in his own day and ours as one of the greatest geniuses (genii?) of All Time, he also had the worst hair and one of the silliest moustaches. He couldn't talk until he was three and after that hardly ever shut up. But these things are always relative, aren't they? I just loved his films – *Battleship Potemkin, Alexander Nevsky* – that's where his genius really lay.

In other news ... The first launderette was opened in Fort Worth, Texas on this day in 1934. It gave Texans hours of endless fun watching their washing go round and only later did the viewing public realize it got their clothes clean too. Bonus! John Yogi Bear, the inventor of television took his inspiration from it and experts today believe that, in seeing a shirt passing the same exact spot every 2.1 seconds is actually more variety-filled than anything on today's nine squillion satellite channels.

April 19

James Mollison was born today in 1905. He was a Scottish aviator and if you've never heard of him that's because all his thunder was stolen by his wife, Amy Johnson. He was actually flying with her when they crossed the Atlantic for the first time, but he might as well not have bothered.

He got his own back later though, by shortening his Christian name to Jim and singing with the Doors, a band that didn't feature Amy Johnson at all, although experts on the band do say that 'You're Lost, Little Girl' may refer to her.

In other news ... Charles Darwin, the famous beagle-breeder, reluctant evolutionist and owner of a horrendous beard, died today in 1882. His last book came out the previous year and was called *On the Formation of Vegetable Moulds*. It has now sold 30 million copies worldwide, is available on Kindle for only £23.94 (price set by publisher) and it spawned an opera, a ballet, a radio series and no less than six movies (two in the silent era). There is talk of another remake starring Sly Stallone as 'Lichen' and Gene Hackman as 'Fungus' with a screenplay, inevitably, by Julian Fellowes.

April 20

One of those great moments occurred today in 1653. Oliver Cromwell. East Anglian squire, Puritan and military whizzkid expelled the boring, pocket lining, selfish b******s who formed the 'Rump' parliament with the famous words 'Do you mean to sit 'til Doomsday come?' Once they were out, he locked the door, put the key in his pocket and walked away. How cool is that?

And where is Oliver Cromwell today?

In other news ... Today in 1770 James Cook on board *The Endeavour* (named after his favourite television cop, Morse) discovered New Zealand. The natives immediately leapt about, sticking their tongues out at him and thrashing his crew at Rugby. The final score was: All Blacks 316, Captain Cook's Fifteen 3.

So disappointed was Cook that he sailed away to find the most boring land in the world – Australia.

April 21

Webster's Dictionary appeared today in 1828. Bob Hope and Bing Crosby were filming *Road to Morocco* at the time and immediately used the book as one of their gags – 'Like Webster's Dictionary, we're Morocco bound'.

The purpose of the Dictionary was to differentiate American English from English English. So instead of 'fortnight'. Webster wrote 'twoweeks' (which looked a bit odd in the 'f's); 'tap' became 'fawcett' (same thing, in reverse) and the definition of 'sonofabitch' was 'rather unpleasant Russian'.

In other news ... Samuel Clemens died today in 1901. He used the pen name Mark Twain, a riverboating term, because many of his novels – *Tom Sawyer, Huck Finn* etc – are set on the Mississippi. Later writers copied the idea – Dick Francis for example called himself They're Off; C.S. Forester used the alias Let Go The To'Gallant and Caroline Graham had the most brilliant nom de plume of all – Another Unlikely Series of Slaughters In A Part Of The Country Where Nothing Ever Really Happens And Doesn't Actually Exist, usually shortened on book spines to Aussiapot C.W. Nerhadae.

April 22

Today in 1971, the Haitian dictator 'Papa Doc' Duvalier, died in his bed. He ran a private army. the Ton-ton Macoute and was generally unpleasant to anybody who crossed him. He was succeeded by his son, 'Baby Doc' and his grandson 'What's Up Doc'.

In other news ... The German philosopher Immanuel Kant was born today in 1724. Among *many* other things, he wrote – 'Act only on that maxim which you can at the same time will to become a universal law.'

What a silly Kant.

April 23

The Man of the Millennium died today (no, not Churchill – that was a piece of propaganda put about by the Conservative Party) when the 'upstart crow' aka the 'swan of Avon', William Shakespeare went to that great theatre in the sky in 1616. Brilliant though his plays and poetry still are, the jury is still out on whether he actually wrote anything other than bills and petty-minded litigation. How, his critics ask, could he have written about –

- Italy, when he'd never been there,
- War, when he'd never been a soldier,
- Shylock, when he'd never even seen a Jew
- Etc
- Etc

People in his native Stratford seemed to regard him as a burgess (his dad made gloves and was involved in local politics) and a fairly stupid one at that; certainly not as a great playwright.

I think he *did* write the plays but I also think his real genius was in pinching ideas, lines, even whole scenes, from anybody careless enough to leave their own work lying around. Hence his immortal line in *Romeo and Juliet* – 'A plagiarism on both your houses.'

In other news ... Well, more of the same, really. In 1879 (and on the very same day Shakespeare died – what a coincidence!) the Shakespeare Memorial Theatre opened in Stratford. The building burned down in the 1920s to be replaced by the monstrosity that still stands.

Will must have been turning in his grave (which is down the road, by the way, in Holy Trinity Church – and it'll only cost you £67.83 to have a look at it [last year's prices – who knows how much it will cost in the season of 2012] **and even more in today's 2020 – and don't get me started on 2025, adjusted for stagflation.**

Oh – by the way. It's St George's Day today.

April 24

William Joyce was born today in 1916. Better known as Lord Haw Haw because of his plummy upper-class broadcasts from Germany during World War Two, he carried American, Irish and British passports. It was the last one that got him hanged since he could legitimately be accused of treason. Nobody took his broadcasts very seriously, but the hangman got the last laugh.

In other news ... A bunch of good ol' boys formed the Ku Klux Klan today in 1866. Their leader was Nathan Bedford Forrest (named after an English football club) one of many ex-Confederate soldiers who couldn't accept they'd lost a war they actually couldn't possibly have won. The Klan went on to have a huge white following in the South preventing blacks from voting, obtaining jobs, education and property rights. Later Klan members extended their targets to Jews and Communists, claiming to represent the land of the free.

April 25

Let's go, children of the fatherland, the day of glory has arrived.' All right, it sounds better in the original French. These are the opening words of the *Marseillaise*, written on this day in 1792 by Captain Claude-Joseph Rouget de L'Isle and put to the music of a marching tune belonging to revolutionary soldiers from Marseilles. It's a rattling good song and knocks the other Six

Nations efforts in international rugby into a cocked hat. It must be the only national anthem in the world that most people know much better than their own.

In other news ... King Edward II was born today in 1284. His dad was kicking seven kinds of ordure out of the Welsh at the time and they demanded a prince who could speak no English to rule over them. Accordingly, the king appeared on the battlements of his brand-spanking-new Caernarvon castle with his baby son in his arms and said 'Here he is, then. A prince who can speak no English.' And so the future Edward II became the first Prince of Wales. He was to go on to a memorable meeting with a red-hot poker, but that's another story. And you have to ask yourself how dim could the Welsh be? You'd think they could have seen that one coming, wouldn't you?

April 26

Terror came from the skies today in 1937 when Hitler's Condor Legion bombed the Spanish town of Guernica. It was target practice for the Luftwaffe in readiness for the Blitzkrieg they would unleash on the rest of Europe two years later. The only other international involvement in Spain's Fascist v Communist civil war came from the International Brigade who were prepared to stand up to the Fascist threat. Pablo Picasso painted a memorable picture.

In other news ... Dancer/stripper/burlesque star Gypsy Rose Lee died today in 1970. She was a brilliant hoofer and a pretty girl, but I like her famous quotation better – 'God is love, but get it in writing.'

April 27

Samuel Morse first saw the light of day today in 1791 before going on to invent the magnetic telegraph and dashing off until he became a mere dot on the horizon.

In other news ... London Zoo opened today in 1818 but only to Fellows of the Zoological Society, who were also allowed to bring their wives and families. Gentlemen were requested not to bring whips in case they lashed out at the odd lion and ladies were warned that spring was the mating season and the management could not be held responsible for anything untoward that may go on behind the bars.

They were presumably talking about the animals and not the keepers.

April 28

This was the day when the Allies got it wrong at Versailles in 1919. Britain, the USA and especially France demanded that Germany (who wasn't even called to the negotiating table) pay £6,600 million for having started the First World War. Four things to note:

1. Germany didn't start World War One – Gavrilo Princip did.
2. Germany was broke and couldn't afford to pay reparations.
3. Woodrow Wilson the American President and John Maynard Keynes the economist wanted a much more affordable reparation settlement. They were ignored.
4. Georges Clemenceau – 'the tiger' – was a vengeful reprobate who consigned his own country to defeat and occupation twenty years later.

In other news ... Benito Mussolini became yet another in a long line of dictators – Julius Caesar, Maximilien Robespierre, the Ceausescus, Saddam Hussein, Muammar Gaddafi, Simon Cowell (oops – typo! sorry!) – to meet their end stickily. It was 28 April 1945 and Il Duce and his mistress, Claretta Petacci, were shot, kicked, spat at and hanged upside down for the benefit of the Italian mob and the cameras.

April 29

Confusing? Coincidence? One of those tricksy little things that the Muse of History (Simon Schama) throws at us now and again? Today, in 1769 Arthur Wellesley, Britain's most brilliant soldier, was born. 120 years later Edward Kennedy Ellington, destined to become a legendary Jazz musician, accomplished the same feat. Wherein the coincidence? Mr Ellington took the name Duke and Mr Wellesley got the title Duke of Wellington. So ... Duke Ellington, Duke of Wellington. Get it?

I shall be asking questions later.

In other news ... The Age of Aquarius dawned today in 1968 when the musical *Hair* opened at the Biltmore Theatre, New York. The songs and dance routines were fine, but nobody cared about that. They all went to see people getting their kit off among cries of 'Vulgar', 'Juvenile', 'Offensive' and 'Good Lord, is that even possible?'

Ah, great days.

April 30

One of the great lines was uttered today in 1945 when Hjalmar Schacht said, 'I wouldn't believe Hitler was dead, even if he told me so himself.' Ain't it the truth? Brilliant, Hjalmar. The man was put on trial at Nuremberg because he had been Hitler's economics minister for a while. He was not, however, a Nazi, as you'd expect from someone who was of Danish descent, brought up in New York and whose middle names were Horace Greeley.

Now, I know, dear follower, that you will be wondering if this is another of my little amusing mis-directions, but, honestly, that is absolutely and totally true.

No, really.

In other news ... John Luther Jones died today in 1900 while driving his locomotive the *Cannonball Express* on the Illinois Central Railroad. He was trying to make up an eight hour delay in the mail delivery at the time and his luck ran out. Not ours, though. In the 1950s, when I was just a lad of sixty or so, they made a TV series for kids starring Alan Hale Junior called *Casey Jones*. If you're my vintage, you'll remember the theme song immediately – AND you'll now be singing it all day. Lucky you and any colleagues or family in earshot.

You can thank me later.

MAY

May 1

> 'Oh, it is the First of May, ooh, it is the First of
> May,
> Remember, lords and ladies, it is the First of
> May.'

Repetitious lyrics? No tune known to man? Yep, it must be an Olde English Folke Songe, all of them obsessed with this date. GIVE IT A REST!!!

Right; I feel better now.

In other news ... On this day back in 1851, Queen Victoria (God Bless Her!) opened the Great
Exhibition of Arts and Industry of All Nations. It was a brilliant triumph, although most of the exhibits were actually British (we are still waiting for the Russian entry to turn up). People said the palace of glass in which it was housed would fall down (it didn't); that London would become a hotbed of prostitution and drunkenness (it already was); that other places would be empty because everyone had gone to the Exhibition (they didn't).

They tried to reproduce the vast excitement of the whole thing in 2000 at the Millennium Dome.

Oh dear.

May 2

The Pink Floyd single *Another Brick in the Wall* was banned today in 1980 by the South African government. And quite right too. Rumour has it that the white supremacists in charge were convinced that the lyrics would inflame black schoolchildren. Actually, of course, they were complaining about the appalling lack of grammar in said lyrics. They *ought* to have read:-

> 'We would rather not have any education.
> We would rather not have any thought control.
> Excuse me, sir, would you mind not attempting to
> punish those children.'

There, that's much better.

In other news ... Lady Nancy Astor was born and died on 2nd May, albeit several years apart.
She is reputed to have asked her son, 'Jakie, is it my birthday or am I dying?' Jakie answered, 'A bit of both, Mum.'

Isn't that cool?

I wonder if Shakespeare came out with the same idea in 1616?

'Faith, sirrah, is this the day I sprang full-formed into this breathing world or will I see the Scythesman spread his black cloak o'er everything?'

To which his daughter Judith may well have replied, 'I dunno.'

I break the habit of this Blog so far to wish a person of my acquaintance a very happy birthday. He is a Renaissance man of the most amazing kind, musician, writer, poet, actor, amazing son and incredible father and all round good egg. In case he hasn't guessed it from that introduction – Taliesin; you know who you are! Many happy returns.

May 3

Margaret Mitchell won a Pulitzer prize for her first novel today in 1937. It was a sprawling Civil War epic called *Gone With the Wind* and was later turned into the Worst Film in History (and I am including *John Carter* and *Titanic* in the list) starring Clark Gable.

Bad luck, Maggie; you can't win 'em all.

In other news ... Niccolo Machiavelli was born today in 1469, one of the most misunderstood Italians of all time (see Benito Mussolini, Cicero, Julius Caesar, Silvio Berlusconi etc etc). His book *Il Principe* (The Prince) written in 1515 is a brilliant description of the *realpolitik* of his day, a time when nobody's virtue was overnice. His works were banned in most European universities and he himself equated with the Devil – 'Old Nick'

– which is *incredibly* unfair. He was, after all, telling it like it was.

He has achieved a kind of immortality though – of all the names of the sixteenth century Italian political scene, which one has come down to us as an adjective? His!

May 4

John Hanning Speke was born today in 1827. I've always felt very sorry for this guy because he was a hugely gutsy African explorer who was eclipsed by pushier people. He discovered Lake Victoria in central Africa and the source of the Nile which people had been looking for for 2,000 years. He was permanently deaf as a result of a beetle crawling into his ear (he cut it out with a knife – health and safety tip; *don't* try this at home!) and got into a bitter feud with fellow explorer Richard Burton (soon to star in *Cleopatra*) over who found what. Speke died on the eve of a debate with Burton as a result of a shooting accident which may have been suicide.

In other news ... Back in 1926 the General Strike began today. It was all about the coal owners, backed by the government, expecting miners to take a cut in wages. The *Daily Mail* (of course!) backed the government and Winston Churchill (of course!) wanted to shoot the strikers. For nine days the miners got a lot of support but after that everybody except the miners slunk back to work.

It is an unproven fact that a *total* strike by *everybody* in the country, including the police, army and health workers, would topple any government in days, perhaps hours. The problem is getting 100 per cent of society to realize that and do something about it.

May 5

As live television goes, it was pretty spectacular. On this day in 1980 a terrorist gang was holding hostages in London's Iranian Embassy and started shooting them one by one. As we all watched agog, black-clad SAS commandos abseiled in through the upper storey windows with tear-gas and guns and killed four

of the five terrorists, releasing all nineteen of the hostages inside.
Fantastic!

In other news ... Napoleon Bonaparte died today in 1821 on
the rocky, volcanic island of St Helena. Rumours that he was
bored to death by Hudson Lowe, the island's governor and
effectively Bonaparte's gaoler, are exaggerated. There was talk
of murder by poisoning, especially in 1840 when his body was
exhumed and shipped to Paris to its current resting place in Les
Invalides. He probably already had stomach cancer or at least
serious ulcers by the time of his final defeat at Waterloo, but it
may also be that he died from arsenic poisoning as a result of
breathing in the pigmentation from his bedroom wallpaper. He
had once written to the Prince Regent asking to be allowed to
retire to Cheltenham which he'd heard was rather nice. On
balance, he was better off on St Helena – if he was bored there,
what *would* he have found to do in Cheltenham?

PS – Napoleon's penis, black and one inch long, was offered for
sale in a London auction house recently. There were no takers.

May 6

Sadly for *The Times* newspaper and Hugh Trevor-Roper, the
historian who said they were genuine, the Hitler Diaries were
exposed as a fake today in 1983. So were the 'Ripper' Diaries
of James Maybrick, the diaries of Samuel Pepys, John Evelyn,
William Defoe and Adrian Mole.
I *knew* it!

In other news ... Maximilien Robespierre, the 'sea-green
incorruptible' French revolutionary and all-round psychopath,
was born today in 1758. He lived next door to another over-the-
top Frenchman, Vidocq, the thief-taker who is often
acknowledged as the world's first detective.
Other famous neighbours include; Marcus Antonius and
Cleopatra, queen of Egypt; Samson Antagonists and Delilah (a
friend of Tom Jones); Lewis and Clarke (who lived in adjoining
tents) and Morecambe and Wise.

May 7

'I let down my friends; I let down my country; I let down our system of government; I let down what was left of my hair' – so said 'Tricky Dicky' ex-President Nixon on this day in 1977.

Unfortunately for the rest of us, the term Watergate with which Nixon will for ever be associated, has been hijacked by journalists for every scandal, major and minor, ever since. Hence, to name but a few – Cowangate; Ramsgate; Margate and Tailgate.

Enough, already!

In other news ... Scientists at Johns Hopkins University today in 1991 were given permission to clone the genes of Abraham Lincoln, the American President assassinated in 1865, to decide whether honest Abe had Marfan's syndrome, the symptoms of which are tallness and long arms.

You know that famous photo of Lincoln with General George B Maclennan (he of the saddle) at an army camp somewhere or other about 1862? Well, I'll grant you (ho ho – Civil War joke) Lincoln looks tall, but on that basis McLennan was *really* short and Mary Todd Lincoln, the President's wife, was a midget.

And nobody's cloning them, I notice!

May 8

Talk about hedging your bets and playing yourself down ... In 1815 Arthur Wellesley, the newly created Duke of Wellington, began his 100 days campaign today which culminated in his great victory at Waterloo. In case he lost however (and he nearly did) he wrote a little package of excuses to Lord Stewart – 'I have got an infamous army, very weak and ill equipped and a very inexperienced staff' ... He might have added, 'So if it all goes tits-up, it's not my fault, all right?'

In other news ... Back in 1947 Henry Gordon Selfridge died leaving an estate of only £1,544. Perhaps he'd spent all the rest at Selfridge's.

May 9

If you're a fan of *Boston Legal*, you'll love the performance by Candice Bergen – 'I'm Schmidt' – and you'll no doubt remember her wowing us all in *Carnal Knowledge*, *Soldier Blue* and *The Wind and the Lion* to name but three excellent films. She was born today in 1946 (impolite though it is to mention a lady's age). Looking at photographs of her today, she is still as gorgeous as ever and must (like Dorian Grey) have a picture of herself in the attic – it's the only explanation. All over the world men are still saying 'Wow!' and women are saying 'Cow!'.

In other news ... Lorenzo il Magnifico (the Magnificent) died today in his native Florence back in 1492. Leader of the Medici clan (early Mafiosi) he was a great patron of the arts, employing (among others) the cream of Renaissance artists Fra Lippo Lippi, Fra Hippo Hippy, Fra Zippo Zippy and the Marx brothers.

May 10

The worst blitz of the Second World War on London hit tonight in 1941. Like all such disasters, figures are unreliable, but there were at least 1,400 deaths and 100,000 incendiary fires all over the capital. The Houses of Parliament were hit, so was St Paul's, the British Museum, Westminster Abbey and every major railway station. The Ministry of Information announced the next day that twenty-eight German bombers were shot down. In fact the figure was a mere eight and one of those crash landed, out of fuel, somewhere in Scotland and had nothing to do with the Blitz at all.

Or did it? The Messerschmidt in question was flown by Rudolf Hess, Hitler's deputy and if you think that's a coincidence you've been reading too much British and Nazi propaganda.

In other news ... One of the greatest generals in the American army died today in 1863 of pneumonia and complications brought on by wounds he received soon after his brilliant victory at Chancellorsville. He was Thomas Jackson, known to all and sundry as 'Stonewall' because of his stubborn steadiness under fire. Ironically, he was shot by one of his own pickets, a terrified teenager who lost his nerve and fired too soon in the darkness while on guard duty at the Confederate camp.

Personally, I wouldn't trust a teenager to point a rifle at me or anyone else for fear they would forget what they were doing and just pull the trigger to hear the bang and see the pretty bullet. It would have been better all round and certainly for Stonewall Jackson if the under twenties had been confined to pea shooters. The Sixth Form at Leighford High are certainly not allowed weaponry of any kind until they have completed at least five terms and then only if they can shoot the 'i' out of the school noticeboard at fifty paces.

May 11

While the English garrison were at church today at Meerut in Northern India in 1857, mutineers of the 3rd Bengal Cavalry went on the rampage, attacking their unarmed white officers as well as their wives and children. The causes of the Sepoy War or Indian Mutiny are still being argued over by historians today but the slaughter of the innocents – it happened again in the House of the Ladies at Cawnpore weeks later – is never justified by a difference of ideologies.

In other news ... Back in 1900 the title of US world Heavyweight was lost by 'Gentleman Jim' Corbett to Jim Jefferies. The fight lasted for twenty-three rounds. Men were really men in those days and of course Gentleman Jim's great grandson Ronnie fought as a budgie-weight before taking to comedy.

May 12

'There was an Old Man called Lear,
Who was born 1812, so I hear He wrote loads of tosh

and was terribly posh,
And always ended the fourth line of any quatrain by
feebly repeating the exact words of the first line, that
repetitive Old Man called Lear.'

In other news ... Bob Dylan, a music legend already, refused to
appear on the Ed Sullivan television show today in 1963 because
it was too 'square'. Isn't it embarrassing how dated that sounds
now, in the era when we dudes are all with the brothers, hanging
with our bitches. The Airmen in the Armstrong and Miller show
have the Carpenter-Maxwells in hysterics every time for much
the same anachronistic reasons. Even Nolan has picked it up
and I heard him say to his mother yesterday, from the
bathroom, 'I done the teeth thing yesterday, blood.' I give the
DI full credit for reaching the landing before collapsing in a
giggling heap.

Although not bywords where music lovers gather, Mrs DI
Carpenter Maxwell and I will be upping sticks and leaving
Nolan to Mrs Troubridge's tender care on 29 June while we
attend the Hop Farm Festival in Kent, where the
aforementioned Bob Dylan will be, if not strutting then at least
shuffling his stuff on the Saturday. We do have rather differing
musical tastes which meet in the middle at The Levellers, on the
Friday – aptly are they named, although that was obviously not
their original intention.

May 13

Pope John Paul II (sweet old boy, ran the Catholic church, you
know the one) was shot today in St Peter's Square, Rome in
1981. His would-be assassin, Mehmet Ali Agea shot him four
times (so His Holiness clearly had friends in high places) in
protest at American and Russian imperialism. Presumably he
also tried to murder the US President on the grounds that he
didn't care for the way the church of Latter Day saints was being
run. You couldn't make it up, could you?

In other news ... Ronald Reagan hit the Presidential (as opposed to cattle) trail today back in 1979. His comment for the Press was 'I used to say that politics was the second lowest profession and I have come to know that it bears a great similarity to the first.'

Who said that guy was losing his marbles?

How did he ever become President?

Twice?

May 14

'Every director,' said Sam Goldwyn today in 1939, 'bites the hand that lays the golden egg.' He may have made more quotable gaffes than anybody else in Hollywood but what did he care? On the same day he bought out millionaires Douglas Fairbanks, Charlie Chaplin and Mary Pickford to take control of the huge United Artists Studio. 'Bring on the empty wallets,' as the man himself almost said.

In other news ... Lionel 'Buster' Crabbe, Navy frogman and oddball, disappeared today in 1956 while diving in Portsmouth Harbour near the Russian warship that brought Soviet president Nikita Khrushchev on a state visit. A headless, handless corpse was found some time later, but it has still not definitely been identified as that of Commander Crabbe. Perhaps one day the former USSR will tell us what actually happened.

May 15

In 1990 today there was an ingenious attempt to hit HMRC where it hurts. The Inland Revenue claimed that Lindi St Clare aka Miss Whiplash owed a great deal of money in back taxes from her time as a brothel-keeper. She refused to pay, for the good of HMRC because, had she done so, they would have been living off immoral earnings. If this was a case in TV's fabulous *Boston Legal* she would have won and we'd all have cheered. As it was, in the real world, the Establishment judge ruled against her. After all, the taxation system in this country has been immoral for years.

In other news ... Today in 1718 James Puckle patented what was probably the world's first machine gun. Gatling and Thompson didn't really need to improve the gun much, but it had to be done because no one could bear the sniggering whenever anyone said, 'Don't you point your Puckle at me!'

May 16

Today in 1929, the very first Academy Awards were presented. The Academy had been created two years before by Louis B Mayer and the first 'Best Film' went to *Wings* from the Paramount Studio (not, as nepotism theorists might have expected, something from MGM). The golden statuette had not yet got the name 'Oscar' - it was still quite formally known as an Academy Award. The story goes that someone - presumably someone who hadn't won one - remarked that the figure, plunging a sword into a reel of film, looked like their Uncle Oscar and the name stuck. I personally smell a PR stunt - in the real world firstly, no one would have heard the remark and secondly, the uncle would have been called Merv or Burt and then I doubt it would have stuck quite so well.

In other news ... Today is the birthday in 1905 of Henry Fonda, who starred in films too numerous to mention. Happy birthday, Henry - I can't say your films lightened my life as comedy wasn't really your thing, or even smiling much, now I come to think of it, but you never turned in a bad performance. In one of those quirks that proves astrology wrong, also born on this day but some years later was Liberace - who really did brighten many lives, my mother's particularly. So thanks to you as well - I hope my dear old Ma has a front seat in all your concerts on the other side.

May 17

Regular readers, please forgive me and new readers don't be put off by this very short blog today. It is the Mem's birthday so not only have I no time to waffle, as breakfast in bed and all the other accoutrements are calling, but as far as Nole, the Count and I are concerned, only one thing important has ever happened on 17th May and that is that she was born. So there we are; no other news, no snippets of history, just Happy Birthday to our very favourite person, with love.

May 18

Budding authors who want to see their opi (opu? which declension is this?) turned into film – beware! On this day in 1832 French novelist George Sand (real name Amantine Dupin) published her book *Indiana*. It took 143 years for it to appear in film form, with Harrison Ford (real name, Harrison Ford) in the title role.

You have been warned!

In other news ... 'It is neither fitting nor safe,' said the Bishop of Rochester today in 1376, 'that all the keys should hang from the belt of one woman.' He was talking about the bad influence of Alice Perrers, who had got her hooks into King Edward III. Where, oh where, was Rochester when the Conservative Party chose Maggie Thatcher as their leader?

Answer: where it's always been. Somewhere in Kent.

May 19

The last great Liberal, William Gladstone, died today in 1898. He was the People's William, the Grand Old Man and there was a huge state funeral to mark his passing. It was downhill all the way after the GOM, right down to whatsisface who currently leads the Lib Dems. No, seriously, I have no idea who that is.

In other news ... Rather depressingly, T.E. Lawrence, aka Ross aka Shaw aka Lawrence of Arabia, was killed today in 1935 swerving to avoid two stupid children swerving all over a country lane on their bikes. He was a fascinating, enigmatic man whose full story will probably never be known. He once said to the poet W.B. Yeats, 'I was an Irish nobody. I did something. It was a failure. And I became an Irish nobody again.'

See what I mean about depressing?

So, to cheer us all up – in yet other news – Dame Nellie Melba, inventor of the peach, or possibly ice cream, cream or raspberry sauce, history is silent as to the exact details, was born today in 1848 in Australia (well, somebody has to be!).

May 20

The Enterprise of England began (again!) today in 1588 when the Spanish Armada set sail from Lisbon. Galleons, galleases, carracks, pinnaces, sakers, falcons, culverins – ships and guns to invade England. The plan was poor. The idea was to sail to the Netherlands (then Spanish), pick up the Duke of Parma and his army and land somewhere on the East coast. If Philip II had mounted a two-pronged attack – Parma from the East and the Duke of Medina-Sidonia from the south – I'd be writing this in Spanish today.

Via con Dios!

In other news ... The Americans got it right today in 1895 when they declared income tax unconstitutional. In fact, *all* taxation is unconstitutional because it is introduced by a minority of people (in Britain the members of the Commons and Lords) which makes the government system an oligarchy, not a democracy. Why, then, do we pussyfoot around HMRC that should, in a true democracy, not exist?

May 21

The 'perfect' murder was committed today in 1924 when Richard Loeb and Nathan Leopold killed 14-year-old Bobby Franks just for the hell of it. Fascinated by the Nietzschean concept of superman, Leopold and Loeb believed they were just that, except that one of them dropped his glasses at the crime scene (ah – always the one little mistake!). The case gave lawyer Clarence Darrow his finest hour and put the cause of antisemitism in the USA back fifty years.

In other news ... Poor old Henry VI died today in 1471. Since he was under arrest in the Tower of London and his opponent, Edward IV, was king, it is likely the sad old bloke was murdered on the king's orders. Henry was a poet and saintly to the point of imbecility. He was the son of Henry V, the victor of Agincourt and all-round tough nut. Isn't it funny how often a great general's kids fall short of expectations? For example, Napoleon's son, the Emperor of Rome, caught a chill reviewing some troops and died.

Talk about chips and old blocks.

May 22

On this day in 1795 the explorer Mungo Park set sail from his native Scotland on a voyage to Africa. It should have been a family affair, but he fell out with his brothers, Hyde and Regents, both of whom went off in a sulk to London.

In other news ... Ex-President of the Confederate States of America, Jefferson Davis, was caught today while on the run from the Union in 1865. He was disguised as a woman and insisted he only ever did this on Thursdays when there was a 'y' in the month and anyway, he was doing it for charity.

May 23

A plea for help. On this day in 1934 bank robbers Bonnie Parker and Clyde Barrow were ambushed by police in Louisiana. In the ground-breaking, heavily romanticized film *Bonnie and Clyde* you may remember a scene just before the ambush in which Clyde is sitting in the car and one of the lenses drops out of his sunglasses. I have found no one who can explain the significance of this. Was it an accident on set and the cameras kept rolling? Does it have any deep-rooted symbolism? If you know ...

In other news ... The Mounties were formed 139 years ago today. Bearing in mind they ride horses, wear broad-brimmed hats and scarlet tunics, it's a wonder they *ever* get their man.

But they do.

May 24

All of my faithful followers will know my views by now on global warming and all the other various doom merchants predicting the end of the world as we know it. It has to be said, however, that the weather over the last few weeks has been none too special (to put it mildly) but as ever, this is nothing new. On this day in 1988, snow fell on the Syrian desert and in Damascus for the first time in fifty years. When I think how demented Nolan becomes at the first flake of the white stuff – and he has seen snow in all of his winters so far – I can only imagine the hysteria among the sand dunes when everyone under fifty was experiencing snow for the first time. I wonder if anyone could remember where they had left their sledges?

In other news ... The first Marx Brothers' film, *Coconuts* aired on this day in 1929. Don't get me started on the antics of Groucho, Karl and the gang, if only because I have watched several minutes of several of their films several times and to date can't find anything to laugh at, although I really have tried, honest. Sorry if that makes me a curmudgeonly old git, but that's just the way it is. The lines are funny – 'What's a thousand dollars? Mere chicken feed – a poultry matter' – but only when you see them written down, or hear them delivered by someone else! Harpo, perhaps.

PS – thanks to my faithful follower, I know now why Warren Beattie loses his sunglass lens. It is in *homage* to *A Bout de Souffle* starring Jean-Paul Belmondo in 1963. See – I knew someone would know!

May 25

Oh, for heaven's sake – global warming again? On this day in 1990 (yes, just two years after snow fell in Syria etc etc) Margaret Thatcher was warning of the dreaded phenomenon and pledging that Britain would cut its emission of carbon dioxide by 30 per cent. A UN report immediately responded that the reduction needed to be at least 60 per cent to have any effect. The report warns of a two degree rise in temperature in the next thirty-five years (in other words, chaps, 13 years from now) and six degrees by the end of the twenty-first century. For all of us who have just shivered through the coldest April and May on record, that somehow seems less scary than Mrs T made it sound in 1990.

This day in history has been one of the busy ones so 'in other news' will just list a few of the absolutely stonking stories which began, ended or took place on this day.

- In 1935 Jesse Owens set five new world records and equalled a sixth all in one afternoon, limbering up for seriously p***ing off Hitler at the Berlin Olympics the next year.
- In 1969, Thor Heyerdahl set sail in a reed boat named *Ra*, hoping to relive the success of his *Kon-Tiki* expedition. I am assuming all went well, but I'm blowed if I remember what happened. I hate sequels, don't you?
- In 1925 the Scopes 'Monkey Trial' began in Dayton, Tennessee. Scopes was accused of teaching the theory of evolution, against the state law. A fascinating case, but a much better film, *Inherit the Wind* starring the wonderful Spencer Tracy and Frederic March. They really do not make them that way any more.
- In 1916, Henry Ford spoke one of the most misquoted lines ever – he *actually* said 'History is more or less bunk.' Still not acceptable, of course, but better than the usual version of 'History is bunk.' And that, of course, is better than the version I often hear muttered by Nine Eye You.
- And finally, in 1768, Captain Cook set off to explore the Antipodes. And we all know how that turned out!

May 26

Today marks the last organized resistance in the American Civil

War, back in 1865. Resistance elsewhere had finished three weeks earlier, but it wasn't until today that the forces west of the Mississippi finally surrendered. Even then, the Confederate navy still held Charleston. Wars are always like this, they end, not with a bang, but a rather drawn out and scrappy whimper. Even today, there are many people who don't know the extent of the Civil War, which left an estimated half a million dead and many more crippled for life. The films based on the conflict have often been rather frivolous – with some notable exceptions, of course. Do I have to mention *Gone With the Wind* again, as the worst film ever made?

Of course I do!

In other news ... In 1940 on this day, the evacuation of the beaches of Dunkirk began with the sailing of the flotilla of 700 or so rather motley craft from the shores of England. As in the war above, this day is often quoted as the day of the Dunkirk evacuation, but it wasn't half as neat as that and you only have to think for a minute to realise that you are not going to get 400,000 men or thereabouts off a beach in five minutes. Even so, it was the most amazing undertaking and remarkably successful. It was just as well for morale that no one knew at the time that no Allied troops would land on French beaches again until D Day on 6 June 1944.

May 27

It isn't often I mention Belgium in this blog and I'm sure most of my faithful followers who have been to the country can understand why. This is why I am so pleased to be able to give it a little bit of a boost today. Don't read on, now – no cheating. You are thinking, that's odd, it isn't the anniversary of the Battle of Waterloo or anything. The poor old geezer is losing his marbles. No, it is .... trumpet fanfare and roll of drums .... that today in 1900, Belgium became the first democracy in the world to elect a government by proportional representation.

Exciting, wasn't it?

In other news ... Vincent 'Mad Vince' Price was born today in

1911. Oddly enough, it was Peter 'Mad Pete' Cushing's birthday yesterday (he was born in 1913). Perhaps surprisingly, they didn't share billing on as many films as you would think, but, God, were they scary? I can feel the hairs standing up on the back of my neck just thinking about it. Both extraordinarily nice men, by all accounts. I'm glad to hear it - it would be very unfortunate if they were just cast to type!

May 28

On this day in 1932, Dutch engineers finished what was then the world's biggest dam (eighteen miles long) which turned the Zuider Zee into a huge freshwater lake. Don't be too impressed, however. In the good old days one little boy held back the sea with a finger in a hole in the dyke.

Hence the old joke - how many Dutchmen does it take to make the Zuider Zee?

In other news ... You know how unfair it is when the wrong person gets the credit? Stand up Dr Joseph Ignace Guillotin, usually credited with the invention of the execution machine of the French Revolution. He was born today in 1738 and, as a member of the Revolutionary Estates General, advocated the contraption on humanitarian grounds because of its speed. The device had already been used in Scotland, Germany and Italy. Just think how peculiar it would sound however - 'Louis XVI was perhaps the most famous victim of Mrs McPherson/Frau Scherendorfer/Signorina Frescobaldi.'

Doesn't have the same ring, does it?

May 29

What is it about 29 May? You might like to stay out of the water tonight because on this day in 1500, Batholomew Diaz, the Portuguese explorer, drowned during a storm off Brazil. Not to be outdone, on this day in 1911, William Schwenk [I kid you not!] Gilbert (as in Gilbert and Sullivan) drowned in his own lake whilst trying to save a child who had got into difficulties. And three years after that, more than 1,000 people drowned

when the *Empress of Ireland* sank in the St Lawrence River.
You have been warned!

In other news ... I've probably said it before in these pages, but it's worth repeating. On this day in 1795 the Virginia Assembly objected to the Stamp Act imposed by the British (i.e. *their* government). The Virginians' argument was basically 'No taxation without representation', James Otis (inventor of the lift) ignoring the fact that because of the state of democracy at the time, well over 95 per cent of the British didn't have any representation either.

Brass neck or what? Why didn't we just declare war on the colonists and have done? Oh, wait a minute – we did.

May 30

Today in 1990, France banned the import of British beef in case it carried the 'mad cow' virus. This was all a storm in a teacup of course, as food scares always are. But it was only tit-for-tat, really. We'd stopped importing their horses by 1565 and it was payback time.

In other news ... One of the most famous voices in cartoon history was heard for the first time today in 1908. Mel Blanc, better known as Bugs Bunny and Daffy Duck, is reputed to have taken one look at the obstetrics team around his cot and said, 'What's up, Doc?'

May 31

Henry Ford has appeared in this blog already, due to his incredible disregard for history in his famous quote. Anyone who was thinking that he might be right should perhaps take his total disregard for the alphabet into account before deciding for certain – today, in 1927, after 15,007,003 models made, the last Model T Ford rolled off the assembly line. What was it replaced by? The Model A.

Go, as Mr Ford's compatriots tend to say in these circumstances, figure.

In other news ... In 1902, the generals commanding the Boers in South Africa surrendered to the British on this day. Kitchener, one of the least deserving 'heroes' in British military history, broke the nation by tactics such as herding the women and children into concentration camps where an estimated 20,000 – one in three of all those interned – died of malnutrition and disease. The peace treaty provided for the eventual self-rule for the Boer republic, with the issue of votes for the native nations to be decided upon at a later date. Just how much later, no one knew at the time and probably a good thing too.

JUNE

June 1

On this day in 1935 the British government hit upon a brilliant idea (the last one before that had been in 1215). It was to test motorists on their driving skills. Now – a little test for you (multi choice to make it easier)

Was the Driving Test:-
1. A good, life-saving idea?
2. The start of the Nanny state?
3. A chance for every family in the land to be bankrupted by the extortionate cost of driving lessons?

In other news ... Sax Rohmer died today in 1959. Who he? I hear you cry. He was the creator of Dr Fu Manchu, the unscrupulous wily Oriental baddie written at a time when you were allowed to regard Orientals as unscrupulous, wily and baddies.

June 2

I absolutely refuse to mention the Jubilee. Oh, dear, I've blown it.

In other news ... Rex Harrison died today in 1990. He was suave and sophisticated and is best known for the following roles:

-   Rex Harrison in *Blithe Spirit*
-   Rex Harrison in *My Fair Lady*
-   Rex Harrison in *Cleopatra*
-   Rex Harrison in *The Agony and the Ecstasy.*

For *My Fair Lady* he won an Academy Award and a Rex.

June 3

The British navy won a victory today in 1665 over the Dutch fleet. Let's not get too smug however – as well as contending with the plague and the fire of London in an eighteen month period around then, we also sat back and watched the same Dutch sail up the Medway and pinch our flagship! Annus horribilis or what?

In other news ... You know how it is, chaps; she says, 'But we spent last Christmas at your mother's' or 'I did let you go to Twickenham'. Well, Edward VIII (the 53-week king) once said 'Of course, I do have a slight advantage over the rest of you. It helps in a pinch to be able to remind your bride that you gave up a throne for her.' He married Wallis Simpson today in 1937.

June 4

Some of you may know that I am something of a cavalry buff, with several hundred 54mm members of the Light Brigade saddled up for the Charge in my attic. 207 years ago today, the first ever Trooping of the Colour took place in Horse Guards Parade. What was great about that is that it was carried out by regiments wearing what was then fighting gear – bearskin on their heads; elephant ivory on their sword-hilts; egret and swans' feather plumes. Sealskin busbies for the Hussars hadn't *quite* come in then, but somebody in the fashion-conscious Horse Guards was working on it.

In other news ... Today in 1937 the worst machine in the history of mankind came into use in a supermarket in Oklahoma. It was the shopping trolley, designed to take the weight off your arms so that you are tempted to spend more. It had the essential features that its modern counterparts still retain:-

- Wheels that never go where you want them to
- Awkward projections that make them jam with others in car parks
- Kiddie seats into which kiddies positively refuse to go.

June 5

It was another dark day for the Kennedy family and the world today in 1968 when Robert Kennedy, seeking political nomination, was shot in the kitchen lobby of the Ambassador Hotel in Los Angeles. His killer was a Jordanian, Sirhan Sirhan (so good they named him twice) but who was the woman in the polka-dot dress who rushed into the street after the shooting, shouting, 'We've got him'? And did she mean Kennedy or Sirhan?

Answers please, on a postcard to:

Conspiracy Theories 4U, 2012 Grassy Knoll, Roswell, New Mexico, Nr Area 51.

In other news ... Today in 1989 the world watched amazed as a trade union organization – Solidarnosc – beat the Communist party in the first free elections in Poland since the First World War.

Nice one, Lech!

June 6

Today was the beginning of the end of Hitler's 1,000-year Reich in 1944 when thousands of British, Americans and even some Frenchmen waded ashore on the Normandy beaches as part of Operation Overlord. This was D-Day, deliverance day and after the shambles of similar operations in earlier wars (Napoleonic and First World, for instance) no one was sure it would actually work. Troops were driven into the shallows by amphibious vehicles known as Ducks and people should have had more faith in them. They appeared as early as 1200(ish) in Russell Crowe's *Robin Hood* (2010). Oh, ye of little faith!

Oh for heaven's sake, 7 Double You You, yes, I am joking. No, they didn't have them. No, I have no idea what accent Russell Crowe is attempting in the film.

In other news ... *1984* hit the bookshops today in 1949. George Orwell's pessimistic view of the future looked forward to a time when two of the worst television programmes in history would actually have a following – *Room 101* and *Big Brother*.

Two little known facts for you now:

Firstly (and obviously when you think about it) Orwell simply reversed the date when he wrote the book and as he was writing in 1948, he called it 1984. If he had chosen the publication date instead, he would have called in 1994. So there were absolutely no clever predictions going on – nothing was going to happen in 1984 and by gum, nothing did.

Secondly, George Orwell was really Eric Blair, father of a future Prime Minister.

Who knew?

June 7

Who was the oldest person to win an Oscar? It was Jessica Tandy, born on this day in 1909. She was 80 at the time and the film was *Driving Miss Daisy*.

In other news ... If, like me, you are all Jubileed out after the events of the last few days, you might like to remember that there was a prequel, on this day in 1977 – the Silver Jubilee of HMEII. It was a novelty then – we hadn't had a Silver Jubilee since George V just managed to squeeze one in before he died. England can take it!

A personal note here – as you all know if you have been paying even scant attention to this blog that I am not a musical person. But even I, even I with my tin ear (and, according to a rumour started by Year 11, a tin leg) could tell that the Jubilee Concert was truly appalling. Listen to me now, you oldies – with the notable exception of Tom Jones – *you can't sing these days, boys; give it up!!* In the case of Cheryl Cole, not even the years can be used as an excuse. She just can't sing. But Paul McCartney, Cliff Richard ... it was appalling. And don't get me started on Rolf Harris* ... The mem has just come in to drag me from the keyboard, having heard my inchoate yelling, so I must sign off, but really ...

> ***For reasons that I cannot go into in mixed company, Rolf Harris has been no-platformed. For ever.**

June 8

Edward of Woodstock, the Black Prince, died today in 1376, probably of dysentery. A brilliant soldier and a tough nut, his death paved the way for the reign of his son, Richard II. who started well by confronting peasants on the rampage in London when he was fourteen. After that it was downhill all the way until he lost his throne, his horse and his life to Henry Bolingbroke.

In other news ... Today in 1969 General Franco closed the frontier between Spain and Gibraltar hoping to ruin its economy. He clearly hadn't noticed that Gib. could be supplied by sea indefinitely, so how was that going to work? It got me thinking, though, about who owns what and how it should all be given back. Britain belongs to the Celts (that's the Welsh, Irish and Scots) so the English can go home. Where's that? Well, some of them have to go to Denmark, Norway and Sweden and others to North Germany. And don't get me started on how the Americans are going to cope.

It is time, however, that we returned the Elgin Marbles to Greece. Their return alone would restore the country's economy overnight.

June 9

My avid reader will have noticed that there was no Blog [yesterday/today?]. That's because it was St Maxwell's Day. Who he? I hear you cry. The original Maxwell was a sailor my grandfather knew, who had so many things that he wanted to do ... you know the rest. Or perhaps you don't. It's by A.A. Milne – I'd look it up for you, but I don't do anything on St Maxwell's Day ...

June 10

722 years ago today, Frederick Barbarossa (the red-bearded) was swept away in a swollen river on his way to the Third Crusade. It was destined, really. There were already so many

egos in that war – Richard the Lionheart, Philip of France, Leopold of Austria, Saladin – and don't get me started on Nicholas of Montferrat! It's difficult to see how Frederick would have fitted in.

In other news ... The first University Boat Race took place today in 1829. Because one team came from Cambridge and the other from Oxford, they naturally decided to hold the contest in London. Why there was no outcry from London University, I can't imagine, unless of course, University College and King's College were slugging it out on the Cam or the Ox; take your pick.

June 11

On this day back in 1509 the marriage took place of Henry VIII and Catherine of Aragon. The poor girl had been kept dangling about, ignored and broke, after her first husband, Henry's big brother Arthur (whose first wife was Guinevere) died. Arthur was only a lad himself at the time and Catherine claimed the marriage was never consummated (which was not what Arthur said, by the way). The whole thing ended in tears, of course, when Henry discovered that his new wife was playing fast and loose with Lancelot du Lac whose illegitimate son Kid Galahad had just been played by Elvis Presley, in the film of the same name.

I hope you're paying attention to all this. I *am* an historian, you know.

In other news ... Ben Jonson was born today in 1572. He was a poet and playwright, well known on the London scene for his short temper (he once killed a man in a duel). Shakespeare referred to him as 'Rare Ben Jonson' but actually he was pretty unique and far more interesting than the rather boring little glover from Stratford.

June 12

Today in 1931, Alfonso Capone, the son of a Neapolitan

barber, was charged with 5,000 offences under America's Prohibition Laws. This man had orchestrated the St Valentine's Day Massacre, made an estimated $100 million from bootlegging, racketeering and prostitution and once beat a man to death with a baseball bat. How mad has the world become when all they could actually get him on was tax evasion (the 1930s equivalent of parking on a double yellow line). I can't help thinking a bullet in the head would have been more appropriate, cheaper and final.

In other news ... Vic Damone, the American singer who had a smash hit with *On the Street Where You Live* from *My Fair Lady* was born today in 1928. I only mention him because until I was sixteen I was convinced his name was Victor Moan and I couldn't help thinking that that was a rather risky handle for a vocalist. **Sadly, Mr Damone is no longer with us; he died in 2018 at the age of 89.**

June 13

On this day in 1842, Queen Victoria became the first royal to travel by train, between Slough and Paddington. There were leaves on the line so part of the journey was undertaken by bus (horse-drawn, of course, in those days) especially after a signal failure on the Stockton-Darlington (three hundred miles away). A spokesman for Railtrack said the problem was regrettable but it should be fixed in time for the queen's Silver Jubilee in 1862 (unless, of course, Prince Albert dies, in which case she won't hold one).

In other news ... Dear old Bazza (Basil Rathbone to you) was born today in 1892. He was actually South African (which wasn't his fault) and he was the best Sherlock Holmes ever, playing the Junkie of Baker Street no less than fourteen times (and beating him every time). He was a suave, deadly film villain too and a brilliant swordsman. Next time you watch the classic duel at the end of Errol Flynn's *Robin Hood* (and you will!) keep a careful eye on Bazza. He's having to slow down and compensate for Flynn, who was no slouch with a sword himself. It would have been too downbeat in 1938 for Guy of Gisborne to have killed Robin, but that's how it should have been.

June 14

Legend has it that after his victory at Marengo today in 1800, Napoleon asked his chef to cook something to commemorate the victory. It has come to be known as Chicken Marengo and ranks alongside other great culinary victories as

- Haddock Grannicus (Alexander the Great)
- Escargots Alesia (Julius Caesar)
- Eggs Agincourt (Henry V)
- Mushrooms Cape St Vincent (Nelson)
- Onions Chickamauga (Ulysses Grant)
- Bananas Merseh Matruh (Erwin Rommel)

Scrummy!

In other news ... Actor and President Ronald Reagan became Sir Ronald today in 1989 when he was dubbed by Her Majesty. Other America recipients include George Dub You Bush and James Earl Jones. Count Basie doesn't count.

June 15

All right, it happened today in 1215 but let me put the record straight once and for all. King John did not *sign* the document called Magna Carta (never *the* Magna Carta, children); he put his seal to it – the official, legal way of agreeing with what the document said (which he didn't, by the way). There is a memorial to JFK and western democracy in the field where all this took place (then called Runnymede or wet meadow, an island in the Thames). Why? Magna Carta had nothing whatsoever to do with

1. America (which hadn't been invented in 1215)
2. Democracy (even though the Greeks had already invented this, they had forgotten all about it by 1215)
3. The rights of Englishmen (Englishmen – not to

mention women and children – would remain downtrodden for the next six hundred years).

All Magna Carta was, was a list of 63 gripes by the barons complaining that King John was trying to knock them into line. Some things in history get distorted – live with it!

In other news ... On this day in 1825, the Duke of York (who was pretty grand not to mention old, according to some accounts) laid the foundation stone of the new London Bridge. He was in Arizona at the time on a fact-finding tour of Third World Countries.

June 16

Today in 1835 William Lovett set up the London Working Men's Association which segued into the Chartist movement some months later. For the record, the six points of the Peoples' Charter were:

1. Universal male suffrage
2. Equal Electoral Districts
3. Payment for MPs
4. Abolition of property qualification for MPs
5. Secret Ballot
6. Annual Parliaments

(not necessarily in that order). What Lovett was trying to do was to establish a true democracy (but note, he dropped women from the equation fairly early as being unworkable). The government of the day found all this far too subversive and the movement failed. Yet today, all of it is law except Annual Parliaments (on the practical grounds of expense and upheaval). So let's have a People's Charter for 2012:

1. No Old Etonians in government
2. No coalitions
3. No involvement in politics by the Lib-Dems

4. Compulsory retirement age in House of Lords of 65
5. No House of Lords.

That makes a lot more sense!

The updated 2020 version reads as follows:

1. **No Old Etonians in government**
2. **No snowflake universities with 'Metro' in their title**
3. **Nobody who is now, or has ever been, a member of Momentum**
4. **No House of Lords**
5. **Nobody who suffers from the condition known as political correctness**
6. **Nobody who is unfamiliar with Hegel's Dialectic.**

And the 2025 update:

1. **No Human Rights lawyers**
2. **No Lawyers**
3. **No Human Rights**
4. **No House of Lords**
5. **Nobody with an IQ of less than 160**
6. **Nobody who does not buy their own clothes and glasses.**

In other news ... Charles Sturt, who discovered most of Australia, died today in 1869. He went to Australia because he was tired of people thinking he was Charles Stuart and being the butt of various unpleasant decapitation jokes.

June 17

The Battle of Bunker Hill was fought today just outside Boston, Massachusetts in 1775. A very dear friend of mine (also an historian) visited the scene some years ago and, as the only Englishman there, was asked who won the battle. Ever the gentleman and with a fine regard for the 'special relationship', he said it was an honourable draw. My friend delighted the

Americans on hand but of course he had his fingers crossed behind his back at the time. Bunker Hill was a British victory.

For the record: GB 1; USA 0 (as all subsequent Rugby matches have proved).

In other news ... Well, it's the same news, really. American soldier William Prescott, at Bunker Hill, is credited with the B-Western cliché original 'Don't fire until you see the whites of their eyes.' Depending on your length of vision, that means you would fire your [flintlock] musket about ten yards away from your victim. yes, you'd probably kill him but behind him were a lot of other blokes like him. Bearing in mind the reload time of a flintlock, that would mean that Mr Prescott himself would die seconds later. Far more sensible advice would be 'Fire as soon as you see anybody coming towards you, then reload like Hell and fire again!'

June 18

It was a 'near-run thing' today in 1815 when Napoleon Bonaparte, arguably the greatest general in history, was defeated by a combined force of British and Prussian troops under Wellington and Blucher respectively. If you're British, you'll claim the British won it; if you're German, you'll claim it was down to the Prussians. If you're French you'll whine and whinge and promise to do better in the two world wars.

Ah ...

In other news ... And on the subject of France in world wars, General Charles de Gaulle urged on his fellow countrymen today to fight on under German occupation in 1940. Gung Ho! you might cry, except that de Gaulle said this over the radio from London, which, while not exactly a safe haven Blitz-wise, was certainly not under the Nazi jackboot.

June 19

On this day in 1829, the Home Secretary, Sir Robert Peel, formed the Metropolitan Police. He had already set up the Irish

Constabulary and made huge strides in reform of the criminal law, making him one of the most brilliant Home Secs of all time. Unfortunately, the boys in blue let him down; of the original 3,000 recruits, most were dismissed within 18 months for drunkenness and bribe-taking.

How often have we heard it? You can't get the staff!

And that was before the Macpherson Report and the general acceptance by the Met that everything said to them by a criminal is 'credible and true'.

In other news ... George Mallory died today on Everest, 1,000 feet from the summit. When asked why he wanted to do it, he famously replied, 'Because it's there.' His body was discovered in 1999 lying face down on the scree. The high altitude and weather had effectively mummified him, and his body was left in situ. The great conundrum of course is – had he already reached the summit before he fell and broke his leg or was he still on the way up?

June 20

Errol Leslie Thompson Flynn was born today in 1909. They don't make them that way any more. Whether he was fighting bad Prince John in *Robin Hood* or the dastardly Surat Khan and the Russians in *The Charge of the Light Brigade* or dying against impossible odds in *The Died With Their Boots On* (probably the worst film title in history, by the way), you always knew exactly where you were with this happy-go-lucky charmer. And how sensible to use his first and last names. Imagine how flat the posters would have looked – *The Sea Hawk* starring Leslie Thompson!

In other news ... Broadway was taken by storm tonight back in 1930 in a show called *Hot Chocolates.* It starred 'Fats' Waller and 'Satchmo' Armstrong, along with 'Jazz Lips' Richardson and 'Baby' Cox. Also in the line-up but not credited were 'Forehead' McCluskey and 'Testicles' Marceaux.

June 21

Prince William was born today in 1982, a bonny 7lb. Like all babies he had blue eyes and his doting father said that the boy had 'sort of blondish hair, but it'll probably turn into something else later.'

He was right – William is now the Hair Apparent.

In other news ... The flight to Varennes took place today in 1791. What's that? I hear my reader cry – a balloon ascent? A Frenchman beating the Wright Brothers to it by 111 years? No, it was Louis XVI's attempted escape out of the clutches of the Revolutionary government who wanted his head. My gripe is this – all the history books refer to the flight to Varennes as though that was Louis' ultimate destination ('If you're tired of Varennes, you're tired of life' – Dr Johnson). In fact, of course – and no disrespect to Varennes, which I am sure is simply lovely – he was just passing through, trying to get somewhere else when he was recognized.

The upshot? A date with Madame Guillotine.

June 22

'When Barbarossa commences,' Adolf Hitler said on this day in 1941, 'the world will hold its breath and make no comment.' Barbarossa was the codename for the Nazi invasion of Russia and, not for the first or last time, Adi got it wrong. The Red Army fought him to a standstill and then drove him back.

Nazi Germany 0; USSR 1

In other news ... Fred Astaire, the brilliant dancer, died today in 1987 at the age of 88. For all you feminists out there, I'd just like to remind you that everything Ginger Rogers did, Fred Astaire did too – only forwards and, despite the rumours, he never wore high heels.

June 23

'Ne ce soir, Josephine,' Napoleon is reputed to have said, which is a shame because Josephine de Beauharnais was a bit of a cracker. As a child of the West Indies, she was the subject of one of Elvis's best-known films, *Kid Creole*, though I have to say I always thought he was a little miscast. Anyhoo, born today in 1763, she was dazzling, vivacious, funny and intelligent, as opposed to Napoleon's second wife, the terribly boring Marie-Louise. What possessed Napoleon to jilt Josephine for Marie-Louise? Josephine didn't provide him with an heir; Marie-Louise did.

Go, as you know our American cousins say for some ungrammatical reason, figure.

In other news ... The British won a classic victory today over Suraj-ad-Dowlah, the Nawab of Bengal. Robert Clive (he of India) was a very strange man, haunted by rumours of cowardice. According to the incomparable Sellar and Yeatman of *1066 and All That* fame, he was a typist in the East India Company. Actually of course he was a brilliant general who just happened to have a City and Guilds in keyboard skills.

Check out his victory at Plassey on this day in 1757.

June 24

Today in 1947 the world officially went mad. An experienced pilot claimed that he saw nine unidentifiable disc-shaped objects in the sky over Washington State. He was either on something or was one of the most brilliant PR men in history. Single-handedly he gave birth to the UFO industry, Greys, Little Green Men, Roswell and Close Encounters of the Highly Improbable Kind. You couldn't make it up.

In other news ... 24 June 1876. Custer 0, Crazy Horse 1. 'Nuff said.

June 25

The older ones among us can remember the balmy days when there was a place off the Adriatic called Yugoslavia. It was ruled by an enlightened despot called Tito, who, while a Communist, refused to bow down to Moscow. Then, on this day in 1991, Slovenia and Croatia declared independence from Yugoslavia and what was once a beautiful country of fine wine (former Yugoslavian red), sun kissed beaches and Medieval castles became a war zone.

What are the Balkans for? Answers please, on a postcard, to Archduke Franz Ferdinand, the Railway Station, Sarajevo.

In other news ... Isn't it funny how Musicals cause such affront? What was created as a fun entertainment usually upsets somebody. *Seven Brides for Seven Brothers* (written by Johnny Mercer who died today in 1976) is based (albeit loosely) on the rape of the Sabine Women. *Showboat* and *Porgy and Bess* exploit black people. *Jesus Christ Superstar* was blasphemous from note one. *Oklahoma* seemed to imply that the inhabitants of the Mid West were a wagonload short of a train. *Carousel* was unkind to Fairground Folk. The list just goes on and on.

And talking of that, why has nobody made a Musical out of *Schindler's List* yet?

Or have they?

More or less, at least in terms of historical inaccuracy. It's called *Hamilton*.

June 26

Peter Lorre was born today in 1904 in Hungary. He starred hysterically in the German film 'M', loosely based on the career of the serial killer Peter Kurten and went on to be decidedly creepy in B-feature horror flicks. His family were well known in showbiz; his mother Annie, was a Scottish tap dancer; his son John was a star of *Dad's Army* on the telly; and his grandson Hugh used to be a comedian but has turned into a really curmudgeonly American house-doctor.

For extra points, dear reader – do you know the name of the cartoon character based on Lorre, a feature of several Bugs Bunny shorts? Well, I'll tell you; I don't want you to get too excited or despondent (depending on whether you know or not). It was Hugo, and the other one was Rocky, based on

Edward G. Robinson. Ah, film trivia – don't you just love it?

In other news ... This was the day when JFK did his bit for US-German relations with the famous 'binliner' speech – 'All free men,' he said, 'wherever they may live, are citizens of Berlin' – which is of course, patent nonsense. As was an earlier part of the speech – 'Civis Romanus sumi' (he meant 'sum' which means 'I am') and again, the parallel is nonsense. 'I am a Roman citizen' *was* a proud boast because half the 'civilized' world had been 'integrated' into the Roman Empire. Much of Europe had been 'integrated' by Berlin, too, in a little thing called the Second World War. So what was JFK saying? Nazi domination is a good thing? Remember, he was chummy with that good old SS Sturmbannfuhrer, Wernher von Braun.

June 27

Charles Stuart Parnell was born today in 1846. He came to dominate Irish politics in the late 19th century, fillibustering in the Commons so that only Irish topics could be debated. Sadly for him, he had a bit of a thing for a married lady, Kitty O'Shea (Tessie's mum) and once the highly prudish Victorians found out about that, it was goodbye from Mr Parnell. He dropped 'Parnell' from his name, dropped the 'a' from Stuart and went on to discover lots of Australia.
Would I lie to you?

In other news ... I would like to apologize for the unforgivable lateness of this Blog which should, of course, have appeared yesterday. We had new software installed by a vegetable who wiped all the old stuff off our computer. In common with various Big Banks, we will of course be paying vast amounts in compensation before falling on our swords to atone for our abject failure.
Would I lie to you?
No – but they would!

June 28

The most bizarre incident in History occurred today in 1950 when an American soccer team beat an English football team 1-0. You must understand, younger reader, that this was a time when *nobody* beat a British team, still less the Americans.

The reason, by the way, why no one has ever beaten an American football team playing American football (as opposed to soccer) is that no one understands the rules.

In other news ... On this day in 1914, a 19-year-old student, Gavrilo Princip, was sitting outside a cafe in Sarajevo. He was a member of a revolutionary gang, the Black Hand and was feeling pretty pleased with himself because he had just heard bombs going off across the city and felt pretty sure that his terrorist group's target, Archduke Franz Ferdinand, must be dead.

Imagine his surprise then when an open-topped car drove slowly past carrying Franz Ferdinand and his wife, Sophie. So what did Gavrilo do? He shot both the car's occupants dead and caused millions more deaths in the First World War.

June 29

Forget the telly and the cinema – you can't beat live theatre. Today in 1603, Will Shaxsper was putting on his Henry V at the Globe Theatre and when the king came on, a real cannon was fired using real gunpowder. So far, so dramatic but unfortunately the place caught fire and burned down. Interviewed by *The Stage*, the playwright said, 'These things happen. You can't write Hamlet without breaking a few eggs.'

In other news ... What possessed this great country of ours to wait until today in 1801 to carry out the first census? Wouldn't 1800 have been neater? Or 1810? Incidentally, for the record, in 1801 there were 26,816 Jedi knights in the country. Where are they now?

June 30

Today in 1520, Montezuma, king of the Aztecs, was killed by

Hernando Cortez's men in Tenochtitlan. He got his revenge however, as anyone who has ever eaten in a tapas bar can testify.

In other news ... What is wrong with this sentence?

> 'At the trooping of the colour today the police arrested a youth who stepped from the crowd and fired a pistol at the Queen.'

Did you spot it? The queen was surrounded by hundreds of her soldiers, men armed to the teeth. They were, by definition, the Household Cavalry and the Guards. Their job when they were formed and when this incident happened in 1981 was and is to protect and defend the monarch. Instead, they let the police do it. What is the world coming to?

JULY

July 1

This is the day in the year when even quite young children realise that *next* Christmas is nearer than *last* Christmas. Detective Inspector Mrs Carpenter-Maxwell and I are currently fortunate that Nolan is not terribly acquisitive, so his Christmas list is usually short and relatively cheap. Metternich's list, on the other hand, runs for two pages and, should we comply with his requests (and let's face it, if we want to keep the skin on our legs, we will) it will keep the shareholders of Pets At Home in Caribbean holidays for the next year or so.

Anyway – on with the blog –

One hundred and sixty-five years ago today the first adhesive postage stamps went on sale in America. For younger readers, I should explain what this experience was. You licked the back of the stamp (and it tasted horrible) before sticking it on the envelope. People who did this a lot used damp sponges at their workstations so that their tongues didn't get all furred up.

For even younger readers, these workstations were called Post Offices and they used to be in buildings (not hidden inside a shop) where you could post letters; even quite small villages had one and most towns had several.

For younger readers still, letters used to be ...

George Sand was born today in 1804. Famous for a long-standing romance with Frederic Chopin. No cause for alarm – George was a woman and Frederic wasn't. Who said Classical music wasn't fascinating?

And talking of composers, another birthday boy today was Hans Henze, he of the musical innovation and elocutionists' tongue twister (not to be confused with Saint-Saens!).

July 2

'General' William Booth of the Salvation Army set up his tent today in 1865 on the Mile End Waste in London's poverty-stricken East End. His hell-fire sermons, tambourines and soup kitchens saved the lives of thousands even before the organization became worldwide. Booth's book *In Darkest England* highlighted the social problems of the day – drunkenness, prostitution, crime. I feel a strange affinity with this man – I own a frock coat like the one he used to wear and at Cambridge, my landlord had met him when he (the landlord of course, not General Booth) was twelve.

This link to history reminds me that I once had my hair cut by George Bernard Shaw's barber, but that, like the Giant Rat of Sumatra, is a story for which the world is not yet ready. Suffice it to say, I destroyed all the photographs, although my sister used to have one, with which to scare the children.

In other news ... Today in 1644, the Battle of Marston Moor turned the tide in the English Civil War. For the first time the hell-for-leather cavalry charges of Prince Rupert of the Rhine failed to break the infantry squares of Fairfax's New Model Army. The Prince's dog, Boye, lay dead on the field and it was rumoured that Boye wasn't a dog at all, but a familiar, an imp sent by the devil to serve Rupert. Oliver Cromwell, whose tactics won the day, had an imp too but his, very cunningly, pretended to be a wart on his chin.

I kid you not.

July 3

American General William Tecumseh Sherman came out with the truth at a speech at the Michigan Military Academy today in 1879. He said, 'I am sick and tired of war. Its glory is all moonshine ... War is hell.' Sadly, later generations didn't listen – hence two world wars, Vietnam etc etc etc.

PS – hasn't Gen. Sherman got the coolest middle name ever?

In other news ... In 1905, Russian troops opened fire of strikers in Odessa. More than 6,000 died which is a tragedy and a terrible harbinger of worse that was to come in 1917. The only good thing to come out of the Odessa steps massacre is Eisenstein's film *Battleship Potemkin*.

Watch that and you'll be a Bolshevik all your life.

July 4

The only memorable thing that happened in the United States today, one hundred and forty years ago in fact, is that Amelia Jenks Bloomer made a speech in Connecticut on behalf of female emancipation and the rights of women to wear what they like on their lower halves. Consequently, thousands of undergarments called Amelias went on sale and enterprising musicians wrote thongs about them.

In other news ... Same news, really. On this day in 1826 two of the blokes who signed the Declaration (see above) dropped dead. One was Thomas Jefferson, the slave owner who nevertheless contended that all men were created equal. And the other was John Adams, father of the much more famous Gomez and Fester.

What are the odds?

July 5

Phineas Barnum was born today in 1819. So when he said 'There's one born every minute' that was a bit of an exaggeration, wasn't it?

In other news ... Today in 1841 Thomas Cook ran the first railway excursion in the cause of temperance. The train ran from Leicester to Loughborough and hordes of women (only men drank apparently in the Midlands in the nineteenth century) shouting 'Down with Demon Drink'. Later campaigns included Railways Against Dichotomy (RAD); Locomotives Against Racial Dichotomy (LARD) and Engines Against Sexual Yobbishness (EASY).

Incidentally, Thomas became the first celebrity Cook in the country*

*Unless you include Captain James.

July 6

It was happy families today in 1189 when Henry II died. As a king he was brilliant, setting up a legal system and kicking the church into touch by putting Thomas Becket, his Archbishop of Canterbury in his place (a vault in said Canterbury). As a dad, though, he had a lot to answer for. His three boys were Richard the Lionheart (psychotic, homosexual, ginger); John Lackland (psychotic, heterosexual, murderer and all-round prat) and Geoffrey (who?). And I haven't even mentioned Henry's queen, Eleanor of Aquitaine who would cheerfully have cut the old man's throat given half a chance.

The story would make an excellent film. Oh, wait a minute – it's already been done. See *The Lion in Winter*. Brill. PS – make sure it's the original with O'Toole and Hepburn. The remake is okay, but it just hasn't got the chemistry.

In other news ... The first all-talkie movie opened today in 1928. It was called *The Lights of New York* and one of its famous lines was 'You ain't heard very much yet, folks, but if you saw *The Jazz Singer* last year, you'd have heard something.'

July 7

A bizarre conversation took place in Buckingham Palace thirty years ago today when Michael Fagan broke into the queen's apartments. Of course it's not protocol to discuss royal chat sessions, but rumour has it, it went something like this:-

> HM: Good Heavens! What are you doing in my private apartments, you nasty little oik?
> MF: I was supposed to meet Bill – you know, Bill Sykes – who was casing the joint, already.
> HM: Aren't you confusing yourself with somebody else? A controversial Semite from London's Underworld, perhaps?
> MF: No.
> HM: Well, what do you want?
> MF: I've got this lad, Oliver his name is, who wants to go straight. I taught him to pick pockets but he's

got real career aspirations and wants to go on
Britain's Got Very Little Talent. Nancy – you
know, Del'Ollio – is trying to help him too, but
Bill's threatening to cut her up.

HM: How can I help?

MF: Got any ciggies?

HM: I'll just call the Old Bill, shall I?

MF: Oh, he is here, is he? Thank God for that, I
thought I'd got the wrong night. Talking of which,
ma'am, any chance of a K? You know, for services
to breakin' and enterin'? Just thought I'd ask.

In other news ... Arthur Conan Doyle, the creator of Sherlock
Holmes, the White Company etc., etc, died today in 1930. But
of course, he didn't. Having thrown himself spectacularly over
the Reichenbach Falls, he'll be back in a minute.

July 8

Percy Bysshe Shelley drowned today in 1822, a great loss to
literature and his friends Byron, Keats and Leigh Hunt.
Actually, without wanting to sound too much of a philistine, he
was a pain in the arse, a rebel for rebellion's sake. He
disapproved of marriage (although he was engaged);
disapproved of meat (you know, like Hitler); disapproved of
royalty (though I bet he would have accepted a K if offered one).

Oh, and he wasn't too fond of water either, but there you
go.

In other news ... The last (legal) bare knuckle fight was fought
today in 1889 when John L Sullivan smashed his way through
75 gruelling rounds to beat Jake Kilrain.

Those were the days (ask Brad Pitt).

July 9

Was this the biggest waste of money in history? Today in 1938
35 million gas masks were provided in Britain against the use of
Phosgene, Mustard Gas and the ghastlies which the 'beastly

Hun' had unleashed in the First World War. You had to carry the damn thing everywhere with you and practice using it for ten minutes a day. Little babies suffered untold traumas by being shoved into whole-body equivalents called Mickey Mouse (and no one knows why – they were about as much like Mickey Mouse as identical twins Danny de Vito and Arnie Schwarznegger). Oh, and the gas mask filter contained asbestos, by the way.

In other news ... Crime writer Dashiel Hammett was jailed today for refusing to testify before Joe McCarthy's House Un-American Activities Committee. He was one of many high-profile targets of McCarthy's Communist witch-hunt which ruined careers and created an appalling element of mistrust. In the land of the free, the only Un-American Activity was that carried out by Joe McCarthy.

Mrs Whatmough models her methods on those of her hero Joe – Nolan and his class recently invoked the fifth over some issues concerning gym kit and won the day. I am so proud of that boy!

July 10

Rodrigo Diaz de Bivar, known as the Cid Campeador (the Lord Champion) died in Valencia today in 1099. For aficionados of the superb Charlton Heston film, I hate to burst your bubble, but he wasn't strapped, dead, onto his horse for one last battle against the invading Almoravid Moors from Africa. He died peacefully in his bed and his body was removed from its tomb four years later to be re-interred by his wife in a Castilian monastery.

He never lost a battle in his life.

In other news ... I'd like to quote from Ted Kavanagh, a wireless script writer in 1947. I make no comment on the quotation at all –

> 'It has been discovered experimentally that you can draw laughter from an audience anywhere in the world, of any

class or race, simply by walking onto the stage and uttering the words, "I am a married man".'

July 11

Thomas Bowdler was born today in 1754. He was the chappie who rewrote Shakespeare and Gibbons' *Decline and Fall of the Roman Empire* without the rude bits (which is odd, because try though I might I've never found any rude bits in Gibbons' *Decline and Fall of the Roman Empire*).

Here is Bowdler's version of a Lenny Bruce performance –

'Hi.'

In other news .... Larry Olivier died today in 1989. That's Lord Olivier to you and me, by the way. Whether you hate his camp delivery or regard him as the greatest actor of all time, he got it absolutely right shortly before his death when he said, 'Acting is a masochistic form of exhibitionism. It is not quite the occupation of an adult.'

July 12

Desiderius Erasmus died today in 1536. He was perhaps the greatest philosopher of the Renaissance and the most revered of the Humanists who paved the way for the Reformation. He also spent most of his time broke and kissing the backsides of various patrons in search of work. He once said, 'I have a Catholic soul, but a Lutheran stomach.'

To steal a deathless line from the girls of Eight Bee Em – 'Yeuw!'

In other news .... The Panama Canal was opened today in 1920. Building it had actually begun in 1881, but, in the immortal words of comedians Smith and Jones, they were delayed because they were waiting for a skip.

2025 update – President Trump says the Canal belongs to

the USA (as does Mexico, Iceland, Greenland, Poundland and London Land).

July 13

Jean Paul Marat was stabbed to death in his bath today by Charlotte Corday. He was a revolutionary responsible for umpteen deaths by guillotine and she was a Girondist. Actually, that's not what happened, not at all*. Ms Corday auditioned for the part of the girl eating a flake in a bath in a special edition of France's Got Talent. Imagine her surprise when she won, got to the studio and found Marat lying there eating the chocolate instead. She lost her cool and stabbed him. Later painters, like David, subtly changed the flake to an ink pot to make it look as though Marat was important.

*For all those who missed *Alcatraz* first time round (not very long ago, but repeats come round faster these days) I do urge you to try to catch it now. The first episode went out this week, so it must still be wandering around on the TV somewhere. When you work out what's going on, kindly let me know! [Update – there is to be no second series, so now *none* of us will ever know what it was all about. Scandalous!]

In other news ... Today in 1923 the British government passed a law banning the sale of alcohol to the under 18s. It is due to come into effect on 1 April 2039.

July 14

The French have a day off today and nobody knows why.

In other news ... Georges Clemenceau, the Tiger, made this momentous statement in 1919 while putting together the ridiculously harsh terms of the Treaty of Versailles – 'It is far easier to make war than to make peace.'

But how would he know? He was pretty crap at both.

Just a quick note for Eleven Are You – if you quote the quote in the recently set essay on the Treaty of Versailles, you

get a mark. If you quote the bit about crap, you get a detention.
Clear?

July 15

Inigo Jones the architect was born today in 1573. At his death,
79 years later, he fell out of a window in the banqueting hall at
Whitehall that he was working on. A colleague standing nearby
saw the dreadful accident and shouted 'Inigo!' Iniwent.

The above joke was first broadcast in *The Seven Faces of
Jim* starring Jimmy Edwards and Ronnie Barker c 1966. The
old ones are the best.

In other news ... Edward Boeing set up his Pacific Aero
Products Company today in 1916. Many years later somebody
wrote a play about him. It was called Boeing Boeing and was set
in his hometown of Seattle Seattle.

July 16

Eighty-four years ago tonight, the Romanov family and their
remaining servants and doctor were shot in the half-basement
room of the so-called House of Special Purpose in
Ekaterinburg. The bodies were burned at the bottom of a
shallow mine pit and reburied nearby. The fact that two of the
Tsar's family's remains were missing gave rise to legend,
speculation and fabrication. Anastasia and her brother Alexei
have been impersonated by dozens of people since that fateful
night. Now their bodies have been found, in the Koptiaki
Woods not far from the rest of the family, which is precisely
what Jacob Yurovsky, the leader of the execution squad had said
all along.

In other news ... Anne of Cleves died today in 1557. You
remember her, she was the ugliest of the wives of Henry VIII
whom he called his Flanders Mare. She passed peacefully away
at the Retired Royal Horses' Home at Tooting.

July 17

Punch or the London Charivari hit the news stands today in 1841. It was brilliantly satirical (even if most Victorian jokes are an average of 84 lines long) with fantastic cartoons and poetry. It is now an unrivalled source of social and political history but sadly the mag is no longer with us, replaced by such literary delights as *Nuts.*

In other news ... Louis 'Satchmo' Armstrong once said (perhaps today in 1954) – 'If you have to ask what jazz is, you'll never know.'
    I, for one, am delighted to remain in ignorance.

July 18

Disneyland opened its doors today in 1955 in California. The brilliant theme park boasted Fantasyland, Frontierland, Adventureland and Tomorrowland. When it moved to Florida and then to Paris, it added other attractions like Orlandoland, ItCostsHowMuchLand and WhyTheHellIsItInFranceLand.
    But we wouldn't miss it for the world!

In other news ... French painter Jean-Antoine Watteau died today in 1721. His name wasn't Watteau at all, but he'd spent several years in England and used 'What-ho?' as a form of greeting. Just as well he wasn't around today, or he'd have been known as Jean-Antoine Wotulookinat.

July 19

The *Mary Rose,* one of Henry VIII's most impressive warships, sank in the Solent today with the loss of nearly all its 450 crew. The jury is still out on why she sank but it has been proved beyond doubt by a careful analysis of the wreck, that it was not because it was sunk by the French. The French gunners were aiming, unsuccessfully, at a barn door at the time.

In other news ... I am barely able to remember the last coronation we had in this great country of ours, but the one I would really have liked to have seen was that of George IV on this day in 1821. Not only did it cost an arm and a leg (see the Olympics 2012) but it was the last time the King's Champion, in full armour, clattered on horseback into Westminster Abbey and threw down his gauntlet as a challenge. How cool was that?

And the scandal was epic too, because the new king's estranged wife, Caroline of Brunswick arrived and hammered on the Abbey doors demanding to be let in as the rightful queen of England. Just brilliant!

> **2025 Update: All right, so I *do* remember the most recent coronation. It was slickly done, impossibly British but unfortunately starred Justin Welby, shortly before he was no-platformed.**

July 20

Valkyrie failed today. Not the film, which was pretty good. But the original plot to kill Hitler in 1944. A bomb was left in an attaché case in the Fuhrer's headquarters at Rastenburg. It went off and killed several but the heavy oak table in the room saved Hitler's life. True, he was shaken, bloodied and partially deaf, but he did survive for another nine months of unparalleled slaughter as the Second World War came to an end. What a shame the first attempt, seven tries earlier, hadn't worked.

In other news ... The Spanish Armada left Corunna today in 1588, delayed by twenty-four hours because of storms. Why, oh why, didn't the Spaniards listen to the weather forecast? And anyway, why were they expecting decent weather in England in July?

On a personal note, most schools break up today for the summer holidays – yes, parents, we do get very long holidays, yes, I know it is a nuisance for you to have to look after your own offspring for six weeks etc, etc, etcetera – and very nice it is too. The weather usually gets worse tomorrow, in readiness for the long holiday and if this happens this year, God help us all.

July 21

The Eagle landed today in 1969 when America became the first country to put its astronauts on the moon. Conspiracy theorists of course claim that the filmed landing took place in a Paramount Films lot and that the moon rock later brought back is actually made of green cheese. As cosmonaut Neil Armstrong said at the time, 'That's one small step for a man, hundreds of backward steps for conspiratorkind.'

In other news ... Not only was he the most brilliant general of the modern world, but he had some great one-liners too. Today in 1798 Napoleon Bonaparte defeated the Mamelukes at the Battle of the Pyramids. He would have another sixteen years of victories like that. And on the day, he said, 'Think of it, soldiers; from the summit of these pyramids, forty centuries look down on you.'

Oh, wow!

July 22

Today, back in 1861, was the first pitched battle of the American Civil War. General Irwin McDowell's Union Troops were defeated by the confederates, thanks largely to the heroic stand made by Thomas 'Stonewall' Jackson's brigade. The North called the battle Bull Run while the South called it Manassas. Then, as now, the capital of the United States was Washington (or Chicago as the South called it) which was, of course, in the District of Columbia (which is actually in Canada and contains any number of Drug Lords).

Who says history is complicated?

In other news ... Sir Mortimer Wheeler died today in 1976. If you don't know who he was, you are under fifty or should be ashamed of yourself. He was the first television archaeologist and always carried out his digs in a three-piece suit and bow tie. He did not have wild flowing hair, a silly hat or a patronizing tone and *never* had only three days to complete an assignment.

July 23

Raymond Chandler hit the world today back in 1888. He was a scrawny kid, kinda small and kinda pink, but he didn't take no nonsense from the broads and got ten to twenty in Leavenworth for refusin' to have his diaper changed.

In other news ... Today in 1940, the LDV ('Look, Duck and Vanish') had their name changed to the Home Guard. They were the boys who would stop Hitler's little game had the Germans succeeded in landing in Britain that summer. As it was, they were the forerunners of one of the most popular and longest running sitcoms of all time.

Although I was always led to believe that the fictional Warmington in which the series was set was actually Goering-am-Zee.

'Go' as our American Allies who didn't join the war for eighteen months would say, 'figure'.

July 24

President Richard Nixon said today in 1969 (of the moon landing) 'This is the greatest week in the history of the world since the creation ... oh, except the week in which Christ was born. And the one that saw the birth of Mohammed and that Buddha guy. Not to mention sliced bread, the wheel and salt and vinegar potato chips.' But we got the general gist.

In other news ... Pierre de Coubertin, called by some the father of the modern Olympics, said today in 1908, 'The most important thing in the Olympic Games is not winning but boasting to the world that your country can host them and then discovering your security is run by the WI and the St John's Ambulance Brigade.'

Prophetic words.

July 25

The Scottish chemist Charles Macintosh died today in 1843. He invented a waterproof outer garment, the name of which is now completely forgotten.

In other news ... Walter Brennan was born today in 1894. He was that toothless old hombre in a million B-feature westerns who wore silly outsize stetsons, was usually drunk and teamed up with the hero. He also used the noms-de-screen of Arthur Hunnicutt, Gabby Hayes and Trigger, Roy Roger's horse.

July 26

'It is uncertain,' wrote Eugene Radin today in 1990, 'whether the development and spread of electronic and computer technology will increase the spread of literacy or diminish the need for it ...'

I told you then, Everyone, and I'm telling you again – the latter. Except that there is never a situation in which literacy is unnecessary. Computers spread literacy like the Nazis spread goodwill and tolerance.

Charles Babbage, may you rot in Hell!

(PS – I hope you're not reading this on a computer ...)

In other news ... Today in 1908 the FBI was set up by Attorney General Charles J Bonaparte (short bloke, conquered a lot of places) to investigate land grabbers and bent big business. Their later boss, J Edgar Hoover, had a natty line in frocks and subsequent agents like Sealey Booth seem to spend all their time on our television screens. And don't even get me started on weirdoes like Scully, Mulder, K and J.

I can remember a time when G Men told you the time and helped old ladies across the street.

July 27

Before I start, let's get one thing absolutely straight. This blog is going to be a completely Olympic free zone. There will be no breast beating when we lose, no hurrahs when we win. I will not be commenting on how totally fabulous the opening ceremony was, how our brave boys and girls are doing in the rifle shooting, volleyball, synchronised swimming or what have you. So – now you know.

Today in 1789, Thomas Jefferson was made head of the new Department of Foreign Affairs of the United States government. This was a *big* mistake. The guy they should have given the job to was Benjamin Franklin, because he had affairs all over Europe already (ask any paid up debauchee of the Hell-fire Club).

In other news ... Congratulations to Gregory LeMond who won the Tour de France today in 1986. As an American, he was the first non-European to win, but check out the name. Obviously, the organizers were a little confused!

Changing his name slightly, he has become an expert on *Bargain Hunt,* one of Detective Inspector Mrs Carpenter-Maxwell's secret guilty pleasures. I'll get it in the neck for letting this one out, but I'm sorry, DI Mrs C-M, the truth sometimes has to be told!

July 28

The History of the Potato is a fascinating subject (no – seriously, it is). Like tobacco, nobody can quite agree when, how or where the very first came to Europe. One theory is that Walter Ralegh (inventor, as every schoolboy knows, of the bicycle) brought tubers back from his back-packing tour of America, planted them on his Irish estate near Cork – allegedly today in 1586 – and intended to feed them to his animals. Gardeners – please don't write in. I know that 28 of July is a rubbish date for planting potatoes, but the books say it is today, so what can you do?

Anyway, I have tried this animal food thing out on my feline companion of a mile, the Count; and whereas he is perfectly happy to nosh any leftover fish, he won't touch chips with a bargepole. So, sorry, Sir Walter, back to the drawing board I'm afraid. Stick with what you know – sea-faring, exploring and knocking off ladies of the queen's bedchamber.

In other news ... Beatrix Potter, creator of *Peter Rabbit* et al, was born today in 1866. I'd like to expose her as a pot-smoking Satanist, blackmailer and arsonist, but alas, she was just a really lovely lady with a great artistic skill and a good line in stories for kids.

Damn!

July 29

There is a famous typo in many books on 'Days in History'. It says that Booth-Tarkington was born today in 1869 and that he wrote *The Magnificent Ambersons*. It *should* of course read that T.M. Ambersons wrote *The Booth Tarkingtons*. It was later serialized as *Highclere Abbey*, which ran for longer than *The Agatha,* by Christie Mousetrap.

In other news ... Poor old David Niven shuffled off the mortal coil today in 1983. The quintessential Englishman, his on-screen officer and gentleman roles, his little moey and charming smile totally belied the fact that he was a quintessential Englishman, with a little moey and a charming smile

July 30

It was the two world wars all over again today in 1966 when England beat Germany 4-2 in the World Cup. England was ahead 2-1 until the last minute when there was a German equalizer (think Arnhem, 1944). Alf Ramsay, the England Manager, said to his boys, 'Well, you've won it once. Now you'll just have to do it all over again and you will. The Germans are knackered.'

And so it proved (see Anthony Beevor's *Berlin*) in 1945.

In other news ... The Parkinson family were in the news again today with the birth of Northcote in 1909. He was the one who coined the idea of Parkinson's Law – Work expands so as to fill the time available for its completion. His dad invented the handle of the condition and his granddad, Michael, is still churning out insurance ads on the telly. And perhaps it is time someone told him he is nowhere as cute as a meerkat (although in his defence he is also infinitely less irritating than a tenor).

> I would like to say that these are yesterday's references to past TV ads, but sadly, they are still with us. 2025 Update: Actually, they are not. Instead, we are bombarded with ads for electric cars (which are expensive to buy, even more expensive to run and will *not* save the planet) and if the ads are to be believed, only work on empty roads in the middle of deserts.

July 31

Cigarette commercials were banned today in 1965 on British television. This was a great shame because they all revolved around the suave and sophisticated and were great fun. Only jet-setting playboys such as Peter Stuyvesant and fascinating blokes in trench coats were ever alone with their Strands.

What do we have now? Tobacco kiosks in supermarkets with shutters down and sad old addicts hanging around pub doorways, inhaling desperately. Vapers exhale more smoke than a Nelsonian ship of the line.

Isn't it about time our kind and caring society made lepers out of other minority groups, like vegans and global warmers?

And, just so you know (as recorded messages constantly remind us), I am not and never have been a smoker, although I was brought up by parents who, on waking, reached for their fags, their glasses and their teeth in that order.

In other news ... Franz Liszt died today. So did Ignatius Loyola and Jim Reeves.

What *is* going on?

AUGUST

Aug 1

Sorry, reader, for this post going up so late, but we all take Lammastide very seriously chez Maxwell and the Precepts of St Bill Gates state quite categorically 'Thou shalt not touch thy keyboard on Lammastide; neither shalt thou post blogs thereon.' So, it really couldn't be clearer, could it? Well, it could be if it was still called Lughnasadh.

Anyhoo ...

Claudius was born today in 19 BC. Obviously, it wasn't 19 BC then on account of Himself not being born for another 19 years. Claudius was one of those brilliant mind-like-a-razor types hiding it all under a limp and a stammer (Kevin Spacey did something similar in *The Usual Suspects*). What Claudius did *not* do was invade Britain in 43 AD (and it really was 43 AD then for obvious reasons). The actual invasion was done by General Aulus Plautius. Claudius turned up after it was all over (typical) to pick up the applause, the statues, slaves, grain, women and everything the Romans had a habit of pinching.

In other news ... Nelson proved he hadn't lost his touch today in 1798 when he attacked and sank Napoleon's fleet in Aboukir Bay, off Egypt. Sneakily, he sailed his squadrons between the French ships and the shore, risking very shallow water. If any other admiral had tried this, his men o' war would have run aground and he would have been court-martialled (see Admiral Byng for something totally different).

Aug 2

Today in 1100 William Rufus (the ruddy) was killed while hunting in the New Forest. There is a stone to mark the spot there today and most people who picnic near it have absolutely no idea who he was. He was a thoroughly unpopular, objectionable git who was probably murdered on the orders of his younger brother.

The moral of this story is – if you are thoroughly

unpopular and objectionable, don't go hunting with your brother's mates. You have been warned.

In other news ... Today in 1918, an Allied Force of British, French and American troops landed at Archangel to try to overthrow the Bolshevik government of Lenin, Trotsky and their good ol' boy comrades. The gambit failed but it was fun while it lasted. My favourite adventurer in this was an English eccentric called Locker-Lampson who went around Russia in an open armoured car machine-gunning everything that moved.

Heigh ho for the open road!

Aug 3

'The lamps are going out all over Europe,' said Lord Grey, the British Foreign secretary today in 1914. 'We shall not see them lit again in our lifetime.' Everybody assumes he was talking about the First World War, soon to erupt with appalling casualties. Actually, recent research has now discovered, he was talking about an indefinite strike by the European Lamplighters' Union.

Duh!

In other news ... On this day in 1926 the first traffic lights (after a Victorian attempt that failed) were installed at Piccadilly Circus. They'd stopped working by 4 August.

Aug 4

The 'war to end wars' broke out today in 1914. The Kaiser, Wilhelm II, said, 'We draw the sword with a clear conscience and clean hands.'

Well ... er ... not really. Although Germany was only one of many countries whose peacetime alliances led them to war, the Kaiser's usual toast with his senior officers on manoeuvres was 'Der Tag' (The Day). What day? The day when Greater Germany would dominate Europe.

In other news ... *Waiting For Godot* opened tonight in 1955 in

London's West End. About half the audience walked out before the end. The others were already undergoing psychotherapy. But then, 'every man has his Sidcup'. How true, Samuel, how true; but I liked you better when you were Archbishop of Canterbury.

Aug 5

'Everybody has a right to pronounce foreign names as he chooses.' Who said that in 1951? The British Prime Minister and war leader Onestop Choochley.

In other news ... George, Lord North, died today in 1792. If you haven't heard of this bloke
1. I'm not surprised
2. You're in good company
3. Neither had x thousand American colonists during the War of Independence.

He was actually Britain's Prime Minister during that whole debacle, and they should all be eternally grateful to him.

Aug 6

The Holy Roman Emperor Francis II abdicated today in 1806. That was because Napoleon told him that he wasn't Holy, nor Roman, nor much of an Emperor. So he threw his toys out of his pram and went home.

In other news ... 'Old Sparky' came to life today in 1890, the first time the contraption was used for an execution. The 'sitter' was the murderer William Kemmler and the place was New York. Under certain conditions, the new 'humane' method could take up to eleven minutes to bring about the death of the convicted felon.

Aug 7

Martha Tabram died today in 1888. She was probably the first victim of the still unidentified serial killer Jack the Ripper aka the Whitechapel Murderer. The Metropolitan Police are a little stretched at the moment with the Olympic security issue, but just as soon as the Games are over, they have promised Press and public they'll be right on it.

In other news ... A UFO was sighted over Basle in Switzerland on this day in 1556. Was it a bird? Was it a plane? Was it Clark Kent? Whatever it was, it was the only thing to have happened in Switzerland since William Tell tried to murder his own son and pretended it was a feat of extraordinary marksmanship.

Aug 8

Richard Nixon resigned today in 1974 over 'errors of judgement' including the Watergate scandal. He remains the only US President in History to have resigned, although an awful lot more of them should have.

In other news ... Talking of which, Vice President Spiro T. Agnew was under investigation the previous year for tax evasion. See? It's everywhere.

Aug 9

Admiral Maarten Harperzoon Troup was killed today in 1653 in a battle with the English fleet off the coast of Holland. I have no comment to make on the man's ability as a sailor (which was considerable) but I have to inform my reader that a recent MORI poll chose him as having the silliest name in History.

In other news ... Brighton opened its first nudist (oops, sorry, naturalist) beach today in 1979. Already dubbed 'Sin City' and the 'Gomorrah of the South', Brighton was assured of the arrival of an army of oddballs in macs (and a handful of naturalists). As an anonymous poster at the time brilliantly put it, 'If God wanted us to walk around naked, we would have been born that way.'

Distressingly, Mrs Troubridge took to naturism in a big

way in response to this innovation. I was away on holiday at the time, but the neighbours opposite took the full brunt, as one might say, of her new hobby and they have never been quite the same since.

Aug 10

One of the world's most important gadgets was patented today in 1889 in Barnsley, not a place usually associated with cutting edge technology. It was the screw-top bottle. So how come it took wine snobs 120+ years to become aware of it?

In other news ... Today in 1949 John George Haigh, the 'acid bath' murderer, was executed at Wandsworth Prison. He was a petty con man who turned to murder for profit but completely misunderstood the meaning of *corpus delicti.* He presumed that if no body was found, a charge of murder would not stick. WRONG! And they found enough of Olive Durand-Deacon's false teeth to convict him anyway, because his chemistry was pretty rubbish as well.

Aug 11

Today in 1932, President Herbert Hoover was the first man in the US to talk sense in twelve years. He said it was time to scrap Prohibition, an unworkable attempt to curb drinking which merely played into the hands of organized crime. Thanks, Herbert – and thanks too for that vacuum cleaner jobbie; excellent. Now the people of America can drink themselves silly (legally) while cleaning their carpets. Not so many thanks for kid brother J. Edgar, though; a Nazi in a frock.

In other news ... Enid Blyton was born today in 1897. Much rubbished in her own time and since for bad literature, she introduced us to a magic world of kids' adventure infinitely better than Harry Potter *and* was a champion of political incorrectness with Golliwogs and Mr Plod the policeman.
Come back, Enid, all is forgiven.

Aug 12

Sorry I'm late with this one, but I've just been out on Leighford Common blasting grouse with my Purdy. All right, none of that is true, but I just want you to be aware of the social class from which I emanate.

Now, to History Business ...

William Blake, poet, artist, visionary and kook, died today in 1827. His poems are pretty good – 'Tyger! Tyger!' etc but his art is *awful*; he was a very poor man's Michelangelo, with flat, derivative scenes mostly from the Old Testament.

In other news ... The last of the Quaggas died in Amsterdam zoo today, in 1883. Zebediah Quagga was out for a stroll in the elephant house when he suffered a fatal heart attack.
     Shame. He leaves no next of kin.

Aug 13

Annie Oakley was born on this day in 1860. If you think the recent Olympic shooting was good, you should have seen this girl. 'Little Miss Sureshot' could hit the thin edge of a playing card at 30 paces. Nobody messed with Annie!

In other news ... and twenty-eight years later, John Logie Baird was born. The Scots are famous inventors and none more so than this bloke. Having designed the world's first television set, he then went on to star in one of the small screen's most lovable cartoon series. For legal reasons, of course, the name had to be changed slightly, so somebody in Head Office came out with the name Yogi Bear.
     They kept in character, though, because he certainly was smarter than the average bear; or human being, come to think of it!

Aug 14

One of the greats of Hollywood died today in 1932. Rin Tin Tin passed away after a long battle with the cat next door. You may remember Rin in such epics as *Dog Day Afternoon, For Whom the Ball Rolls, Straw Dogs* and *Reservoir Dogs*. He caused controversy when he was turned down for the part of Old Yeller on the grounds of his colour and Black Beauty on the grounds of his species. He was technical adviser on Kevin Costner's *Dances with Alsatians*, itself a remake of the French classic *Chien Autumn*.

His favourite director was Anthony Mann, hence RTT's description of himself as 'Mann's best friend'.

In other news ... The Colony of Virginia held its first legislative assembly today in 1619. They had powers granted to them by the British crown to pass certain local laws. What a golden opportunity! And what did they do? Passed laws against drinking and gambling.

Moral: You can take the Puritans out of England, but they'll probably all move to Virginia.

Aug 15

The Scottish king died today in 1057. I can't mention his name of course, in deference to my thespian friends (there's never been a law against that, by the way) but you know who I mean. Shakespeare made up the twaddle about the murder of Duncan, the mad wife, the tendency to see daggers everywhere and the marching wood of Dunsinane. And he pinched most of that from a bloke called Hector Boyce who went on to write the screenplays of several of the Hamish Macbeth (oh, damn!) series.

In other news ... I had to put my cane away today in 1977. Actually that's a bit of a metaphor. I never used the cane in my life (my private life is my private life) and note how sneaky it was of the government to ban corporal punishment in schools during the summer hols – how *are* you enjoying the hols, by the way, parents? Tired of the little dears yet? They *can* be tiring, day after day, can't they?

167

Where was I? Oh yes – I didn't use the cane, I just used the old, tried and tested methods of plugging little delinquent Johnny into the mains, hanging wilful Sarah up by the hair and forcing the whole of Seven Bee Oh to eat a Jamie Oliver school dinner.

Parents – don't try this at home.

Aug 16

This was a date (along with 7th December) to live in infamy. Today in 1819 a peaceful, unarmed crowd of weavers and spinners turned up on St Peter's Fields, Manchester, to listen to the demagogue Henry Hunt talk about universal suffrage, a right we now all have and take for granted. The size of the crowd (perhaps 60,000) alarmed the local magistrates who sent in the Yeomanry to arrest Hunt. In the ensuing chaos, the cavalry attacked the crowd, who stampeded in panic and eleven people were killed, with hundreds more seriously injured.

When I visited St Peter's Square, Manchester, some years ago, there wasn't a single plaque or dedication to those victims visible. I believe there is now – and about time. The authorities of the Cottonopolis should be ashamed of themselves.

And they've at last made a film about it now; shame it's dreadful.

In other news ... Elvis Presley died today in 1977. Or did he? I mention this only because he is probably the most frequently sighted corpse in history, so perhaps today in 1977 has no significance whatever. He would be seventy-seven now (... *is* seventy-seven ...?) so might not be rocking quite so much as he did. Swivelling a hip when it is not one's own is generally accepted as being pretty tricky.

Aug 17

One of the most bizarre murder stories of all time came to light today in 1980 when baby Azaria Chamberlain went missing from a camp site at Ayers Rock in Australia. Azaria's mother,

Lindy, claimed that a dingo took the sleeping child from their tent. The body was never found.

There were three problems with this case –

a) The Chamberlains belonged to a religious sect and that made them suspect in the eyes of many people.
b) Ayers Rock was an ancient Aboriginal site linked with child sacrifice and finally,
c) The Green Lobby said that dingoes were harmless, God's creations etc etc and would not take a child.

After umpteen trials, hearings and years of anguish to the Chamberlain family, the case has finally been closed. My message to the greens out there?

> The dingo did it. They are vicious wild animals and have attacked humans both before and after Azaria Chamberlain.

In other news ... Rudolf Hess, Hitler's deputy, died today in 1987. He had been the only prisoner in Spandau Gaol, Berlin for years, having been sentenced to life for Nazi war crimes at Nuremberg. He was alleged to have strangled himself with electrical flex hooked onto a window frame. the only problem with that is that he was physically incapable of doing it, having had a stroke previously. All the evidence points to murder but because of the man's reputation, no serious investigation ever took place.

Aug 18

Robert Redford, born today in 1937, tells the best put-down story about himself of any Hollywood icon. He was driving around LA one day at the height of his fame when he saw a crowd of people waving at him and calling. He thought he'd give them a treat, so he pulled over and wound down his window, at which point an excited young woman said breathlessly, 'Robert Redford, you asshole!'

In other news ... And talking of assholes, Temujin died today in 1227. Better known as Genghis Khan (the Great Lord) he brought terror and destruction to millions from his native Mongolia to the Black Sea. Adolf Hitler was recently voted the most evil man of all time – by people who'd never heard of Genghis Khan!

And by the way, if you ever want to see probably the worst film ever made starring a Hollywood A-lister, watch *The Conqueror* starring John Wayne as Temujin. Oh dear!

Aug 19

Coco Chanel was born today in 1883 and made a name for herself in fashion design. Which was odd bearing in mind the orange up-and-down hair, red nose, wide check trousers and huge shoes she always wore were something of an acquired taste.

Perhaps it was the water-squirting buttonhole that did it.

In other news ... Today in 1934 the German people went to the polls to vote whether Adolf Hitler should be allowed to use the title Fuhrer. 38 million said yes. The 4 million who said no were shot.

Aug 20

Back in the *Chariots of Fire* year (1924) today, Scottish athlete Eric Liddel famously refused to run the 100 metres at the Paris Olympics because the race was run on a Sunday and he was a devout Christian. If everybody had done that, doing nothing but praying on Sunday, I doubt there would have been any Olympic Games at all.

In other news ... Today in 1839 Louis Daguerre and Isidore Niepce showed the Academie des Sciences in Paris how their brilliant photographic techniques worked to bring us the world's first effective photographs. They were called Daguerrotypes as opposed to Henry Fox Talbot's Talbottypes and George Eastman's Eastmanotypes. Which goes to show, in photography, it takes all types.

Aug 21

Today was the day, in 1858, when General Sam Browne (he of the Cavalry) designed a brilliant new sword belt. He'd lost an arm during the Indian Mutiny of the previous year and found drawing his sword difficult because swords were slung by two loose straps from a waist belt. The 'Sam Browne' carried a sword frog that held the weapon close to the hip and could be drawn with one hand.

They don't make them like that any more.

In other news ... The first Cadillac, the Rolls-Royce of American car design, appeared today in 1902. It had so many additional features ((four wheels, steering wheel, doors etc) that they immediately wrote a song about it – Knick Knack Cadillac.

Aug 22

527 years ago today the last king of England to die in battle, Richard III, was killed at Bosworth. Now, I know what you're thinking. How can a blogger who calls his bike White Surrey after Richard's horse be anything other than biased on this subject? Let me assure you that as a professional historian I am fully aware of the strict importance of objectivity and scrupulous impartiality.

I am also fully aware that the Duke of Richmond, who beat Richard at Bosworth (unfairly) was the most disreputable, rancid, vengeful and paranoid ruler ever to sit on the English throne.

See?

In other news ... Oliver Lodge, the physicist, died today in 1940. Or, since he was an ardent believer in spiritualism, did he?

Aug 23

Napoleon wrote to his adopted son Eugene de Beauharnais

today in 1810, saying 'My principle is: France before everything.'

Well, everything except grabbing everybody else's country, selling his own troops down the river, Creole women and, as the great Sellar and Yeatman put it in *1066 And All That*, 'standing like *that*'.

In other news ... Alaric and his Visigoths destroyed Rome today in 410, ending seven centuries of culture and civilization. Actually, that's not quite true. There was a great deal of culture and civilization outside the Roman Empire and in terms of their cruelty and rapacious greed for territory, the Romans were the Nazis of the ancient world.

Aug 24

Mount Vesuvius erupted today in 79AD and the ash and molten lava completely engulfed the towns of Pompeii and Herculaneum. The loss of life was of course appalling but every volcanic ash cloud has a silver lining. Today we know immeasurably more about 1st century Rome than we would have done if there had been no eruption and Pompeii and Herculaneum just grew into modern towns, replete with bars and pizza joints.

When the Mem and I visited Naples (before you ask, don't bother ...) we visited both Pompeii and Herculaneum and though both are wonderful, enjoyed the latter the most. There were no school parties (a huge plus as far as I am concerned) and in fact, no other visitors but us. At Herculaneum, you really get the feeling of the depth of the ash, as it is literally carved out of the ground and also many of the original tools left by the original excavators in the eighteenth century are lying next to their abandoned work, as if the archaeologists have just popped out for lunch. Two historical goose pimple moments for the price of one!

In other news ... Now, this will upset people, but George Stubbs was born today in 1724. It's not his birth that will upset you, but my next statement. George Stubbs was not the world's greatest horse painter. All his animals have tiny, greyhound-like heads and virtually no ears. And when they're galloping, they've got all four hoofs off the ground. Don't try that at the Riding School! There! I've said it. And, do you know, I feel a lot better.

Aug 25

Today in 1919 the first scheduled flight took place between London and Paris. A siffleuse (female whistler) was employed to entertain the (presumably terrified) passengers. It was very noticeable that everyone wanted to fly *from* Paris *to* London and not vice versa.

In other news ... 'Is Paris burning?' Hitler asked today in 1940 as the Wehrmacht took the French capital. This was an 'in' joke really. Napoleon, a century and a half earlier, said 'If I made one mistake in my life it was not to burn Berlin.'

Aug 26

I tell this story to my GCSE classes and AS aspirants every year. At Crecy on this day in 1346, Edward III and his son the Black Prince took on a French force twice their size and destroyed it. At one point when the Prince's flank was under heavy attack, he sent a messenger to his father asking for reinforcements. The king said, 'Let the boy win his spurs' and sent him nothing. Why do I tell this story to my GCSE and AS candidates? Because the Black Prince was their age – 16 – at the time.

They don't make them like him any more.

In other news ... I shouldn't tell half my readers about this in case they create a copycat situation. Today in 1970 women went on strike in New York and the city stopped. Don't have nightmares, chaps, but can you imagine? No tea in bed? No full English? No cleaned house, ironed shirts, washed car, walked dog, gourmet dinner ... I can't go on because this is a family blog!

Aug 27

When told he was about to die today in 1635, the Spanish playwright Lope de Vega said, 'All right, I'll say it: Dante makes me sick.'

I'm made of much sterner stuff. I don't need to wait for my death bed to shout from the rooftops – 'I don't like semolina!'

Gutsy cutting edge or what?

In other news ... Today in 1987, a Chinese girl who had been brought up by a family of pigs returned to normal life after three years training.

How can anybody who has read *Animal Farm* be surprised by this?

Aug 28

Charles Darrow died today in 1967 (although some sources say it was tomorrow). Who he? I hear you cry. Let's just say he went to jail, did not pass go and owned a great deal of property in Mayfair and Whitechapel.

Got it now? That's right. He was the inventor of *Cluedo*.

In other news ... Today in 1850 the Channel telegraph cable was laid between Dover and Cap Gris Nez.

Why?

Aug 29

The British flagship *The Royal George* went down in the Solent today in 1782 with the loss of over 800 people, several of them civilians. The *George* was careening (that's having its bottom scraped – don't snigger, Seven Eff Dee) when it rolled over. Rear Admiral Richard Kempenfelt was on board and went down with it. Who was to blame? The ship's captain and first officer, neither of whom were on board at the time. Were they punished? Of course not, the British navy let them off! What an institution!

In other news ... On this day in 1918 6000 British policemen (there weren't any women - sorry ex **WPC Carpenter**) went on strike today over pay. They were warming up for a much bigger effort the following year.

Aren't our policemen wonderful? Not necessarily ...

Aug 30

Denis Healey was born today in 1917. Who? I hear you cry, gentle reader. He was a Labour **MP**, Cabinet Minister and Chancellor of the Exchequer with the bushiest eyebrows in politics. He was mercilessly lampooned by the impressionist Mike Yarwood with the immortal phrase 'Silly Billy'.

Sadly, he departed this vale of tears in 2015.

In other news ... Marcus Antonius committed suicide today in Alexandria in 30BC. He'd just lost a war against Octavius Caesar and not even his famous wife, Cleopatra, could shake him out of his depression. He did 'what's fine, what's Roman' (that's your actual Shakespeare) after his bodyservant refused to kill him with his sword.

Aug 31

Caligula, the Roman Emperor who was even madder than all the rest, was born today in 12AD.

And a lot of people wished he hadn't been!

In other news ... Van Morrison was also born today, but a little bit after Caligula - in 1945, in fact. I only mention the fact because I don't understand the cult of (white) Van man. We have Van Gogh, Van Johnson, Van Morrison, Van Diesel, Van Dango.

It's all Vanity, I suppose.

SEPTEMBER

Sept 1

A.A. Milne got it right today in 1919 with his comment on chess. He said 'It is impossible to win gracefully at chess. No one has yet said "Mate!" in a voice which failed to sound to his opponent bitter, boastful and malicious.' How much better it would be to say 'Chum', 'Pal', 'Me Ol' Mucker'.

In other news ... the first supermarket in Britain opened today in 1951. It was called the Premier and it ushered in a whole raft of phrases in the English language that hadn't been heard before e.g. 'This is a colleague announcement'; 'on special offer today we have' and 'spillage in Aisle 14'.

Sept 2

Sorry I missed yesterday, dear reader (I have done it now, so scroll backwards to read it) but as the new term looms I had to pop in to see Mr Gove* to put him straight on a few matters. And don't worry – he won't be bothering any of us again.

*Mr Gove, back in the day, was the Minister of State for Education. Now, it's a four year old called Gavin Williamson. 2025 Update: Now it's Bridget Phillipson. What? I hear you cry? A woman in the Cabinet?

Now, to more important matters ...

Ho Chi Minh (he of the city and the trail) made a nuisance of himself in Hanoi today in 1945 by proclaiming the Democratic Republic of Vietnam. As Commie as apple pie, he upset the Japanese, the French, the British and finally the Americans, leading to the deaths of thousands.

Why can't people realize that foreign powers lording it over them know best? (See Owain Glyndwr, William Wallace, Toussaint L'Overture, the Founding Fathers, Geronimo, Jomo Kenyatta etc etc etc).

In other news ... Louis Napoleon surrendered to Kaiser

Wilhelm of Prussia today in 1870 after being thoroughly trounced in the Franco-Prussian War which would see the new state of Germany emerge the following year. Masters of efficient and organized warfare, the Prussians had 26 railway lines to transport their troops to the killing fields. The French had one.

Go, as both the French and the Germans say today, figure.

Sept 3

This was the day in 1939 when Britain and France declared war on Nazi Germany. An apprehensive Britain crowded around their wireless sets to listen to the Prime Minister's announcement. They needn't have worried, though. As Alan Bennett pointed out in *40 Years On*, 3 September was also the date of Cromwell's great victory over the Scots [Battle of Dunbar 1651, but you knew that already I am sure] but Hitler didn't know that. But then there were a lot of things Hitler didn't know (have you *read* Mein Kampf?).

In other news ... Richard Plantagenet became Richard I of England today after years of fighting with his father, Henry II and brothers Geoffrey and John over the succession. Bearing in mind that this rather unpleasant psychopath spent only six months of a ten-year reign in this country, one wonders why.

Sept 4

As cool things go (I understand from my students that this is archaic young-person speak meaning 'impressive', 'to be admired') West German Mathias Rust has to take the biscuit (which is late Medieval speak for 'win the race' 'achieve the utmost') when he flew through Russian airspace on this day in 1987 and landed his light aircraft in Red Square. Just think what he could have done if he'd had the Luftwaffe with him!

In other news ... 'How can you bear to go further?' asked Lin Ze-Xu, the Chinese Imperial Commissioner in a letter to Queen Victoria today in 1839. 'Selling products injurious to others in order to fulfil your insatiable desire?'

It's not generally known that 'Vic the Kraut' as the Underworld knew her was a hopelessly depraved junkie and ran a Prostitute and Bootleg racket that made Al Capone look like Mother Theresa. And isn't it a bit rich of the Chinese lecturing *us* on crap, substandard goods and cheap knock-offs?

Sept 5

The longest-running comedy in the world – *No Sex Please – We're British* – closed in the West End today in 1987 after a 16 year run and 6671 performances. That's the one where the policeman did it – in the nude.

In other news ... 'I have not ruled out the possibility of one day coming to power.' Who said this today in 1991? Was it:

1. Richard M Nixon
2. Tony Blair
3. Grand Duke Vladimir Kirillovitch
4. Simon Cowell?

Sept 6

The Marquis de la Fayette was born today in 1757. Dashing, brave, romantic and with the obligatory white horse, he fought for the Americans during the War of Independence. The *really* smooth move came from Colonel C.E. Stanton when his troops arrived in Paris in
1917. He visited the great man's tomb and said, 'Lafayette, we are here!'
Just brilliant!

In other news ... There was a glitch in the computer network in Paris today in 1989 when 41,000 people guilty of traffic violations like illegal parking and speeding, received letters charging them with extortion, prostitution and murder.
The Ministry of Justice at once apologized and sent all

41,000 to the guillotine on the grounds that there's no smoke without fire.

Sept 7

'Grandma' Moses was born today in 1860. Her real name was Anna Robertson and she began painting at the age of 78. In her 90s, she took up break-dancing and won three gold medals in the 1952 Geriolympics, most notable leading the over Eighties Nudist Trampolining team to victory.

Go 'Grandma'!

In other news ... The battle of Lepanto stopped the Ottoman advance into Europe today in 1571 when a Christian fleet led by Don John of Austria destroyed the galleys of Ali Pasha, releasing thousands of galley slaves in the process. Ali Pasha was killed and his head presented to Don John as a souvenir.

For a brilliant poetic account of the action, see _Battle of Lepanto_ by G K Chesterton. See, I've made it easy for you by adding a link (possibly ...)

Assuming this link works (which let's face it is unlikely) you will be transferred to a page from Untermeyer's splendid _Modern British Poetry,_ from an edition when the wonderful Gilbert Keith was still among us – don't be confused by the lack of date of death, he is not still alive at almost 140, more's the pity. He actually died in 1936. He was, as they say, no age. If you are unfamiliar with his poetry, which is a little neglected these days, I really urge you to read some. You'll love it, I promise.

Sept 8

This review appeared in the _Field and Stream_ magazine in 1961 -

> 'This pictorial account of the day-to-day life of a gamekeeper is full of considerable interest to outdoor inclined readers ... In this reviewer's opinion, the book cannot take the place of J.R. Miller's _Practical_

Gamekeeping.'

This was of course a review of D H Lawrence's *Lady Chatterley's Lover* and we must assume that *Field and Stream* was being tongue in cheek about the whole thing. *Bums and Tits Weekly* was rather more forthright, of course -

> 'What a load of $%^&*!!! The ^&%$£^* is pretty good but we also had all this %"**& about gamekeeping thrown in.'

In other news ... Today in 1916 President Woodrow Wilson promised American women the vote. He later withdrew the offer on the grounds that the First Lady, Mrs Woodrow Wilson, had him in a side head mare at the time and he wasn't thinking straight.

Sept 9

King James IV of Scotland was killed at Flodden today in 1513. The sneaky little non-Sassenach took the opportunity to invade England while Henry VIII was away fighting the Battle of the Spurs in France.

The moral of this story? Don't be a sneaky little non-Sassenach*.

> ***Nicola Sturgeon, this one's for you. 2025 Update: I have literally no idea who runs the SNP today, rather like most Scots people.**

In other news ... Chaim Topol was born today in 1935. I think he's a first rate actor and no doubt a lovely man, but oh dear, *Fiddler on the Roof*? It's just awful, nearly as bad in the film stakes as *Gone With The Wind* and, the greatest turkey of all, *The Sound of Music.*

Sept 10

Sevastopol fell to the British and French armies today in 1855 after an 11-month siege. It should never have taken that long but the Crimean War holds the record for the biggest number of military cock-ups in history (Ten Zed Oh – I will be needing more detail in your holiday projects, which I assume most of you busy writing today ahead of our first lesson together since July which is Period 3 the day after tomorrow, if I recall my timetable accurately). If you're ever in the Crimea, go to the Panorama, a huge circular building lit by natural light which shows a single day during the siege in a 360-degree montage of paint and 3D models. It is an astonishing work of art. Imagine how much better it would have been if the Russians had won!

In other news ... Today in 1962, Martin Luther King said, 'I want to be the white man's brother, not his brother-in-law.' Think about that. It's really clever.

Sept 11

'People of the same trade seldom meet together but the conversation ends in a conspiracy against the public or in some diversion to raise prices.'

Adam Smith wrote this in *The Wealth of Nations*, published today in 1776. The Mother Shipton of his day, Smith was of course talking about bankers in the twenty-first century.

In other news ... Oliver Cromwell ordered the slaughter of 1,500 rebels at Drogheda on this day in 1649. Among them were women and children. The irony is that Cromwell today is regarded as one of the more tolerant of Puritans. It's just that Papists (i.e. the Irish) didn't come within the remit of his compassion. So next time you read something extolling the virtues of the Lord Protector, just bear Drogheda in mind. Oh, and Wexford too, because he did the same thing there.

Sept 12

And so it begins, dear reader. Yesterday, for me, was what I call All Hell Day in which I enrolled the new Year 12, all of them convinced their GCSEs have been wrongly marked. I told them all to go and see that nice Mr Gove and gave them a few tips on urban terrorism to jolly things along.

Today is the start of the Michaelmas Term, as we used to call it when all members of staff in schools had Oxbridge degrees (that ended in about 1733).

William Boyd died today in 1972. Who he? I hear you ask. He was the hero of my childhood, better known as Hopalong Cassidy. He didn't hop very much but he sorted out the bad guys with his fists and his six-gun and rode on a white horse called Topper. He also wore a black hat (Hoppy, that is, not Toppy) which caused confusion because the good guys always wore white hats. What was the world coming to?

In other news ... Maurice Chevalier was born today in 1888. He was an actor, acrobat and all round thoroughly twinkly old charmer. What a pity his *Thank Heaven for Little Girls* would be totally misconstrued today.

Sept 13

An indelible stain was left on American prison authorities today in 1971 when 1,500 New York State militiamen opened fire on protesting prisoners in Attica Jail near Buffalo. Ten guards and twenty-nine convicts were killed.

In other news ... 'Black Jack' Pershing was born today in 1860. He was a gung-ho general of the Great War and a famous cavalry officer before that. He also introduced military music to the American army having seen the British Guards Division in action.

What a shame he couldn't teach them to march as well.

Sept 14

Two extraordinary women died today in car crashes, fifty-five years apart. The first was the dancer Isadora Duncan whose neck was broken as her trailing scarf got caught in the rear wheel of her Bugatti in 1927. The second was the gorgeous Princess Grace of Monaco (aka the actress Grace Kelly) whose sports car went off a road and plunged 120 feet over the edge. Both accidents happened near Nice and both women were already legends before Fate intervened.

In other news ... Jack Hawkins was born today in 1910. The gravel-voiced actor always played officer or authority figures, from Gideon of the Yard to General Allenby. One of his last films was as General Picton in *Waterloo* by which time throat cancer had robbed him of his marvellous voice. What a loss.

Sept 15

The first British robot appeared today at the Model Engineering Exhibition in London in 1928. It immediately downed tools and refused to work until suitable arbitration had taken place vis-a-vis the workplace, an afternoon tea break and a tanner extra in the docket.

In other news ... Titus Oates was born today in 1649. In case you're wondering who he is, he is the bloke who invented breakfast cereal and just popped out for a little while from Robert Falcon Scott's snowbound tent in the Antarctic.
So now you know.

Sept 16

Alexander Korda was born today in 1893. Though Hungarian, he emigrated to Britain and made a host of rattling good yarn films like *The Drum* and *The Four Feathers* extolling the virtues of the British Empire and the Raj. Winston Churchill got him a k; they don't make directors like that any more. My good lady, the DI, tells of many a Sunday afternoon when she was a child when she and her mother were taken hostage by her father to watch *The Four Feathers* just one more time. When stressed, she still can lapse unconsciously into a rendition of several minutes of the dialogue, absolutely word perfect, even after all this time.

In other news ... Tomas de Torquemada died on this day in 1498. Posterity has been pretty kind to this man, whose name is largely unknown today. He was the architect of the Holy Inquisition which saw the torture and execution of thousands of innocent people all over Europe. He deserves to be up there with Hitler, Stalin, Idi Amin, Pol Pot etc. Spread the word. He wasn't Mr Nice Guy.

Sept 17

Hector Berlioz triumphed on this day back in 1837. His *Requiem* performed in Paris had a choir of 200, 110 violins and 16 tympani (and the Brass section couldn't sit down). His music is great (although he couldn't play a single instrument properly) but his *hair!* Look at portraits of him. Even allowing for the exaggeration of contemporary cartoonists, Berlioz had the silliest hair in Classical Music.

In other news ... *HMS Resolution*, Britain's first nuclear submarine was launched today by the Queen Mother in 1966. It was the first time that a Royal had used the well-known family Scuba-diving skills and the old girl hardly suffered the Bends at all.

Jolly good show, Your ex-Maj.

Sept 18

'What dreadful hot weather we have! It keeps me in a continual state of inelegance.' So wrote Jane Austen to a friend today in 1796. This quotation is for my old enemies in the English and Geography Departments really. Geographers please note – global warming as far back as 1796, so stop whingeing and spreading tales of doom and panic. Englishers – why is your darling writing such tosh (see *Persuasion, Northanger Abbey* etc etc) when she should have been writing about the extraordinary French Revolution happening only a few miles away at the time?

In other news ... Another one for the English Department.

Samuel Johnson was born today in 1709, in Lichfield (shame!). He is heralded today as one of the first lexicographers in the world. In fact, he was a neurotic bossy-boots with a nervous tic who is famous only because an equally neurotic bossy-boots – James Boswell – wrote down every word the great man uttered. To see Johnson put firmly in his place, see Robbie Coltrane's performance of him in *Blackadder III*; perfect!

Sept 19

'Try stubbing out a cigarette with both feet while rubbing your back with a towel.'

This action describes –
1. Discovering a fire in Pudding Lane, London, in 1666 and attempting to prevent its spread
2. Being Lord Mayor of London 2012
3. Doing the Twist 1960
4. Auditioning for the part of James Bond 1960-2012?

Answer please to: Mr C. Checker (oh, damn; I've given it away!)

In other news ... Lesley Hornby was born today in 1949. She's better known as Twiggy and was *the* face of the Sixties modelling scene. Amazingly, she's still going strong today and still looks great. Unlike the other Sixties models, Stringy, Skinny and Skeletal who, frankly, are beginning to show their age.

Sept 20

Today in 1959, Nikita Khrushchev was denied access to Disneyland for security reasons. The *actual* reason was that none of the Mickey Mouse actors (Mickey Mice actors ...???) wanted to hug him.
　　And who can blame them?

In other news ... It's a perfect day for sailors today. In 1519, Ferdy ('I tell you the world is round') Magellan set sail from

Seville with a little fleet of five ships. And in 1580, Frankie ('Yes, it is, and it all belongs to England') Drake came back with five ships having circumcised the globe.

All teachers reading this will know that the above is not a typo – in this specific case it is a quote from an exam paper from Leavon Clutterbuck (not his real name) of 7 Eff Pee, c. 1983.

Sept 21

Bonnie Prince Charlie (the young chandelier – see yesterday's post) won a battle at Prestonpans today in 1745. I mention this for three reasons:

1. It was the only battle Charlie ever won – finally losing the one with booze in 1788.
2. It inspired a brilliant folk song about the English commander General Sir John Cope – 'Hey, Johnnie Cope, are you waulking [awake] yet?'
3. Isn't it great that our wonderful country has a place in it called Prestonpans?

In other news ... John Loudon MacAdam was born today in 1756. He went on to become one of the great road engineers of the Industrial Revolution using gravel held together by tar. It has since come to be known as TarAdam and you see it everywhere.

P.S. It usually melts in the summer, to the unaccountable amazement of local councils everywhere.

Sept 22

Robert Walpole, the Whig leader whose career was a byword for corruption, moved into the new house for Prime Ministers, Number 10, Downing Street, today in 1735. Next door was one of his cronies, the Chancellor of the Exchequer (oh, no, wait a minute – that was Walpole too). Everybody else in the street was so appalled by their new neighbour that they not only left, they had their houses demolished.

In other news ... It was today in 1980 that Idi (The Last King of

Scotland) Amin told Uganda's 80,000 Asians they had forty-eight hours to leave the country.

The whites were given six minutes.

Sept 23

There was a furore today in 1987 when ex-Intelligence officer Peter Wright's book *Spycatcher* was published in Australia. The man was a whistle blower, spilling info he should not have done under the Official Secrets Act. MI5 went into a tailspin, the *Sunday Times* was held in contempt of court and the government went ape-faeces.

How different it all is today. We all know the name and address of MI5's M (it's Judy Dench, by the way – cunningly doubling as an actress); it no longer matters about your sexual orientation if you want to be a spy (as long as it's more or less Nor'Nor'west) and they advertise in the paper – 'Top Spies Wanted. No Experience or Qualifications Necessary'. What bothered me about the *Spycatcher* Case was the fact that a man we to whom trusted the security of the country could be photographed wearing such a silly hat.

In other news ... The blueprint for all modern police forces was seen for the first time today in 1912 when Mack Sennet's Keystone Cops hurtled at high speed across the screen, wearing summer regulation straw helmets and huge moustaches. It is still going on today, minus the straw helmets and huge moustaches in every constabulary in the country.

Oops; I think I'd better delete this because the Mem (who some of you will know is a Detective Inspector of some repute) has threatened to take away my computer for forensic analysis.

Also, I should apologise for the lateness of this blog. Today's downpours have finally been too much for the roof of Casa Maxwell and water is pouring merrily into the bathroom and heading down the stairs. The builder is on his way, but I hope he comes soon because my finger is getting tired plugging the leak.

Sept 24

Today in 1877, a rebellion of Japan's samurai was put down by the government. You've probably seen the story filmed as *The Last Samurai* with Tom Cruise. It's not bad historically, except that the country offering military advice to the Japanese government was Germany, not America. The idea was that the samurai were an armour-wearing anachronism, whose code of Bushido (the way of the warrior) was hopelessly out of date. Why was it then that Bushido was still there in the 1940s which explains the appalling brutality meted out by the Japanese to British, Australian and Dutch prisoners of war? And why has Japan's 'enlightened' government never apologized for that?

In other news ... Otto von Bismarck, the Prussian Chancellor, came out with one of his great bon mots today in 1862. 'The great questions of the age,' he said, 'are not settled by speeches and majority votes, but by iron and blood.'

Right on, Otto. The result? Germany 0; Rest of the world 2.

Sept 25

In a scene reminiscent of dear old Leighford High any day of the week, 1,000 men of the 101st Airborne Division with fixed bayonets marched into Little Rock High School today in 1957 so that nine black children could take their rightful places in class. Outside the school, a mini-riot ensued. Where did all this happen?

That would be America, the land of the free.

In other news ... The first blood transfusion took place today in 1818 at Guy's Hospital in London, but everybody was rather ... oh, negative about it.

Sept 26

Dan'l Boone, the famous American frontiersman, died today in 1820. He was buried with his favourite span'l.

In other news ... The Holy Alliance was formed today in 1815 between the powers that had defeated Napoleon. Russia, Austria and Prussia all put pen to paper and agreed to come to each other's aid even if it meant putting down democratic risings. Britain, who had done more than anybody else to beat the French, refused, our man at the Congress of Vienna, Lord Castlereagh, calling the whole thing a 'piece of sublime mysticism and nonsense'.

What *would* he have made of the EU?

Sept 27

One of the most famous letters in history landed on the desk of the Central News Agency today in 1888. It began 'Dear Boss' and ended 'Yours truly, Jack the Ripper'. It sparked the greatest and longest-running murder industry in the world.

In other news ... Some books will tell you that Engelbert Humperdinck died on this day in 1921. Please go to your local library TODAY and alter this in any relevant book. Engelbert Humperdinck sang Britain's entry in this year's Eurovision Song Contest. Mind you, he didn't look well ....

Sept 28

The First International met today in London in 1864. Its leader was the indefatigable Karl Marx (whose brother, Harpo, by coincidence died on this day in 1964). Among Marx's best-known lines -
- Religion is the opium of the people.
- You have nothing to lose but your chains; you have a world to win.
- Friedrich, can you lend me ten bob 'til week Thursday?
- Oh, my bum is killing me!

In other news ... Herman Melville, the author of *Moby Dick* died today in 1891. The story, about a man's obsession to get revenge on a great, white whale, is an allegory on any number of levels and is quite brilliant. It would be unpublishable today because:

1. Greenpeace would object to whaling.
2. Captain Ahab has only one leg – health and safety implications.
3. The book has too many silly names for modern readers – Queequeg, Nantucket, Pequod.
4. The title is obscene and would have to be changed to Moby Male Member – mind you, the alliteration works!

Sept 29

The first automatic telephone answering machine was tested today in 1950 by the Bell
Company. The recorded message went like this:-

> 'Hello Caller, You have reached the Bell Company. I'm afraid no one is here to take your call at the moment so if you'd like to leave a message after the Bell stops ringing, someone will get back to you. If you have a query about other Bell Company services, Press Button A. If you have a query about your bill, Press Button B. If you need to talk to a person ... er ... oh, dear, I'm afraid all our buttons are busy right now. Please try later (about 1985).'

In other news ... George Bernard Shaw, Irish playwright, raconteur and general smartarse, turned down a peerage today in 1930; not on any socialist principles, but because he realized how silly the title Lord Shaw of Ayot St Lawrence would sound.

Sept 30

The Prime Minister, Neville Chamberlain, flew into Croydon airport today in 1938 with a scrap of paper. It contained Adolf

Hitler's promise to invade no more countries after Czechoslovakia. He called it, optimistically, 'peace with honour', echoing Benjamin Disraeli's phrase after the Congress of Berlin in 1878. Unfortunately, Hitler was not of the calibre of the statesmen Disraeli sparred with and the scrap of paper was worthless. Was Chamberlain aware of that? Almost certainly, but years of Appeasement had made Britain unwilling to face up to Europe's bully-boys.

In other news ... Today in 1630, John Billington was the first to be executed for murder in New Plymouth, beginning a fine tradition that Americans still continue to this day.

OCTOBER

Maxwell's History of the World in 366 Lessons

Oct 1

Kaiser Wilhelm II (he of the silly moustache and pickelhaube) gave orders to his generals today in 1914 – 'It is my royal and imperial command that you ... exterminate first the treacherous English and ... walk over General French's contemptible little army.'

He was obviously a tad confused. General French *was* an Englishman, despite his contrary surname and the German generals clearly weren't listening carefully enough. They didn't exterminate the British because the 'contemptibles' stopped them at the Marne. I know I don't have to remind you of the score: Britain 1, Germany 0.

In other news ... Louis Leakey died today in 1972. He was the brilliant, self-taught anthropologist who discovered 'Lucy', a partial skeleton in the Olduvai Gorge in Tanzania. His findings put him at odds with almost every other anthropologist over the issue of who was descended from whom. You and I, for example, dear reader, are descended from homo sapiens by way of homo habilis and all points south. Year Ten at Leighford High School are descended from homo deeply-stupidicus and, according to his mother at least, the testicles of Henry Guttersnipe (not his real name) haven't descended at all. Although why that should excuse the late delivery of his most recent essay, I am at a loss to explain.

Oct 2

Can we get this straight once and for all, please? Today was the day in 1780 when John Andre was executed by the American colonists as a spy and working with the traitor Benedict Arnold. Andre knew the risks he was taking and was unlucky; that's Africa. But Benedict Arnold was not a traitor. Today, thinking Americans equate him with Adolf Hitler, Vlad Dracula and Attila the Hun, but he was actually doing his duty as a British subject, which all American colonists were. it was *all the rest* who were the traitors, whatever gloss the slave-owning, line-pinching Thomas Jefferson tried to put on it in the Declaration of

Independence.

In other news ... 'There are many reasons why novelists write, but they all have one thing in common – they need the money.'

(With sincere apologies to John Fowles, who said something totally different today in 1977).

Oct 3

Elias Howe died today in 1867. Who he? I hear you cry. He was the chappie who invented the sewing machine and (unusually for pioneers in any field in the past) made a mint out of it (not literally, Seven Eff Em – he wasn't *that* clever). They even wrote a song about the sewing machine – 'A sewing machine, a sewing machine, a girl's best friend. If I didn't have my sewing machine, I'd go round the [expletive supplied by Seven Eff Em] bend.'

They don't make them – or write them – that way any more.

In other news ... Postcodes were introduced in Britain today in 1959. Yes, I was surprised by that too. It was the start of the End of Civilization, of course and another step on the road to 1984 (naturally!). What happened to those glorious postal triumphs of the past when General Wilson of the First World War fame addressed an envelope to himself as 'The Ugliest Man in the British Army' (that was all he wrote) and it actually reached him.

Oct 4

Karl Baedecker, the German publisher, died today in 1859. This is quite remarkable and an astonishing piece of research on my part (eat your heart out, Eric Hobsbawm RIP). Because during the Second World War, the Baedeker raids hit the very cities in Britain listed by Baedecker nearly a century earlier. Coincidence? I think not! Clearly, Karl Baedecker was an early member of the Nazi Party. Has nobody else noticed this?

In other news ... As a kid I could never understand how the

gadget developed by Paul Zoll at the Harvard Medical School actually worked. It was designed to control heartbeat and, as far as I knew, was called a peacemaker. I couldn't understand how a six-shot revolver carried by cowboys could be any help at all in that respect. That's why I became an historian rather than a cardiac surgeon and probably just as well.

Oct 5

'Gangin' doon, Geordie, gangin' doon, to the toon where the power lies.'

The unemployed men of the Tyneside shipyards marched to London today in 1936. Jarrow had a 66 per cent unemployment rate and, wearing flat caps and blankets, 200 men set off to a rousing cheer. Everybody en route gave them tea and sandwiches, even the odd pint of beer. The hunger march didn't achieve much but it was a far cry from a similar march in 1817 when the Blanketeers set off from Manchester to protest about poverty. They were met by the army at Stockport and dispersed.

In other news ... Monty Python's Flying Circus first appeared on the BBC today in 1969.
Why?

Oct 6

Two men died today in the electric chair in Florida in 1941. Their names were Frizzel and Willburn.

In other news ... You don't mess with Basil II, Holy Roman Emperor. Today in 1014 he trounced the Bulgarian Army of Tsar Samuel and ordered that the prisoners should be blinded. Every hundredth man was to have one eye spared so that they could find their way back to the Tsar. Ah, the good old days.

Oct 7

Desmond Tutu, the Archbishop of Cape Town, was born today

in 1931. He's a brilliant guy, loved and respected throughout the world. I must share with you, though, the unexpected thing for which he will always be remembered. If you are of average university ability, you will acquire a 2.2 (or Lower Second) degree; now affectionately known as a Desmond.

In other news ... It was today in 1905 that one critic, viewing the works of Matisse in Paris, said, 'A paint pot has been flung in the face of the public.' He should have stuck around. Since then, 'art' has got much, much worse.

Oct 8

Count Metternich (no, not the furry version, the real one) was appointed Foreign Minister in Vienna today in 1809. He stayed in office until 1848 as 'the coachman of Europe' directing and manipulating everybody with his craftiness and army of secret police. That's why I gave that cute little bundle of fur the name all those years ago – I can recognize a serial killer when I see one.

In other news ... Chicago almost burned to the ground today in 1871 when Mrs O'Leary's cow knocked over a lantern in a barn in Dekoven Street. Under interrogation, using the good cow, bad cow (and incidentally giving the name to an otherwise anonymous disease) system we've all seen so many times, the animal confessed to being a serial arsonist, admitting to similar fires in London (1666), Warwick (1694) and London again in 1861.

Oct 9

'Che' Guevara was shot dead by the Bolivian army today in 1967. Let's forget how ludicrous it was that a self-centred, rather useless asthmatic medical student could become the icon of a generation (mine) appearing on posters and tee-shirts without number. Let's have a closer look instead at the Bolivian Army. They shot Butch Cassidy and the Sundance Kid too. Is nobody *doing* anything about this?

In other news ... Today in 1897, Henry Sturmey drove away from Land's End in a 4.5hp Daimler with the intention of being the first person to drive to John O'Groats – 929 miles. Today, because of roadworks, contraflow, traffic cones and utterly unnecessary 50mph speed limits on open roads, that journey would take five days.

Turn around when it is safe to do so.

Oct 10

Charles Darwin published what he considered to be his major opus today in 1881. It was called *Formation of Vegetable Mould through the Action of Worms with Notes on Their Habits.* Just a reminder about other immortal works penned by the greats: Harriet Beecher Stowe's *The Outbuilding belonging to a family Relative Whose Name was Thomas*; Karl Marx's *A List of the Principles and Beliefs of People Who Believe in Complete Equality*; Robert Graves's *Myself, Tiberius Claudius Drusus Nero Germanicus* and finally Peter Benchley's *The Mandibles of a Large, Pale Predator Fish and Its Homicidal Habits.*

Darwin's book was later filmed as *Tremors and Its Many Sequels.*

In other news ... Thelonius Monk was born today in 1920. For years I thought his name was Felonious and that he was probably a defrocked priest. His crime? He virtually invented bebop.

'Nuff said.

Oct 11

Jean Cocteau, poet, artist, filmmaker and all-round brilliant wit died today in 1963. Of all the cool things he ever said, my favourite must be 'Tact consists in knowing how far we may go too far.'

Ain't it the truth?

In other news ... And talking of wits and great lines, how about this today in 1991 from Auberon Waugh (whom I actually met once) – 'Politicians can forgive almost anything in the way of abuse; they can forgive subversion, revolution, being contradicted, exposed as liars, even ridiculed but they can never forgive being ignored.'

Takes one to know one, Aub!

Oct 12

The first non-religious piece of music was published today in 1609. It was *Three Blind Mice* and isn't it an odd thing to kick off Showbiz with? Burt Bacharach, who wrote it, dined out on the royalties for the rest of his life.

In other news ... Aleister Crowley was born today and spent the rest of *his* life telling everybody what a beast he was. His phone number was 666 (as opposed to the Pope's which is VAT 69); his favourite dish was devilled kidneys and he liked children but couldn't eat a whole one.

Oct 13

The Turin Shroud, allegedly the cloth wrapped around Jesus' crucified body, was finally exposed as a hoax today in 1988. This shouldn't have surprised anybody. For centuries, the Catholic Church had been making money out of exhibiting the chains of St Peter, the finger of St Anthony and the foreskin of Sister Ursula (oh no, that can't be right!) and all of those were fakes, so why not the shroud?

The *real* miracle is how did a brilliant fourteenth century artist fake the thing in the first place?

In other news ... The Queen, God Bless Her, made her first broadcast to the nation today in 1940. She was only 14 and said, on *Children's Hour* 'We know, every one of us, that in the end all will be well.'

And the old girl's been calming us all down ever since. **Update 2025: RIP Elizabeth II. Vivat Rex!**

Oct 14

Cliff Richard was born on this day in 1940. If you've seen recent photos of the man, you'll know this has to be a typo. He was clearly born in 1990.

Or does he have a painting of himself in the attic ...?

In other news ... The world came to an end today – although Mother Shipton never noticed it – in 1969. The ten bob note was replaced by a nasty-foreign-looking coin called a 50p. I'd have been happier had it been called a 120p, but you can't have everything.

Oct 15

Yesterday I told you the world came to an end in 1969 but there are those who argue it happened today in 1582 when Pope Gregory XIII changed the calendar, thereby losing nearly eleven days. Millions of people therefore died before their time. Has the Vatican apologised for this, the greatest mass slaughter in history? Has it, Heaven!

In other news ... Virgil was born today in 70 BC, which is astonishing really. How old must he have been at the OK Corral when he faced the Clantons and McLowerys with brothers Wyatt and Morgan and Doc Holliday?!

Oct 16

It was a great day for executions today. In 1555, Bishops Latimer and Ridley went to the stake in Oxford for their religious beliefs. And in 1793, 'the Austrian woman', Marie Antoinette, went to the guillotine in Paris. Somebody drew her in as she travelled in her tumbril on her way to the Place de Guerre. She was thirty-eight and looks a hundred. How are the mighty fallen?

In other news ... Angela Lansbury was born today in 1925.

Check out (as her countrymen would say) this amazing lady – she was brilliant in *The Court Jester*, gorgeous in *The Three Musketeers*, a national treasure in *Murder She Wrote*. She is about to tour Australia with the great James Earl Jones in *Driving Miss Daisy. And* she's related to a British Labour Leader, George Lansbury.

They don't make them like her any more.

And recently, aged 95, she has dazzled on stage as Madame Arcati in *Blithe Spirit*.
2025 Update: RIP Angela, 1925-2022.

In a personal note, I would like to wish a very happy birthday to my very good friend M.J. Trow. I am reluctant to give his year of birth – like Cliff Richard, I suspect him of having a portrait in the attic – but he is an all round nice chap and altogether much too modest, so, Happy Birthday, M.J. Trow, from your staunchest fan.

Oct 17

John Wilkes was born today in 1727. This man took on the corrupt government of George III single-handedly and almost toppled it. Womanizer, gambler, member of the notorious Hellfire Club and all-round pain in the Arras, you couldn't help but love him.

And no, Ten Aitch Why, he *did not kill Abraham Lincoln*!! How many more times do I have to say it?

In other news ... Charles II was defeated by Oliver Cromwell's Ironsides at Worcester today in 1651. About 20,000 people claimed later it was *their* oak tree Charles hid in before nipping across to France. The king had the last laugh, however. When he got his throne back nine years later, Cromwell was already dead. Undeterred (get it?!) they dug him up and dragged his body around the streets of London. Where was Health and Safety?!

Oct 18

I must just interrupt my daily trip down Memory Lane to register the winning of the Man Booker Prize – for the second time – by Hilary Mantel. Now, Ms Mantel won it the first time by writing a novel about Thomas Cromwell. She won it the second time by writing a novel about ... Thomas Cromwell. Is it only me who sees a pattern here? Next year, if we *all* write a novel about Thomas Cromwell, we're all bound to win. Incidentally, old TC was a thoroughgoing b*****d, but in that sense no worse than anybody else in the Tudor period.

Back to the blog –

Canaletto was born today in 1697. With a name like that of course he couldn't paint anything but canals. So Michelangelo called himself Bibletto; Stubbs was professionally known as Horsetto and Geronimo Monteverdi the master forger was Falsetto. Any Italian painting a still life was Stiletto.

In other news ... Lord Palmerston died today in 1865 with the famous words 'Die, my dear doctor? That's the last thing I shall do.'

And do you know, it was! Spooky, huh?

Oct 19

George Cornwallis surrendered to the American Forces at Yorktown today in 1781. They re-enact the moment for tourists every year, except that there are a few things missing ... like the colonists' German allies, the troops of the Marquis de Lafayette, a lot of Dutch and Spanish cash to buy weapons and mercenaries. Oh, and half the French navy.

Apart from that, of course, Yorktown was a fair fight.

In other news ... Auguste Lumiere, inventor of the cinematograph, was born today in 1862. His eldest boy was known as Son of Lumiere.

Oct 20

Richard Burton died in Trieste today at the age of 69. It was 1890 and the explorer was one of the giants of Victorian England, never fully recognized (despite a knighthood) because of his penchant for translating the *Kama Sutra*, naughty bits and all. He was the first Englishman to visit Mecca during the Hajj (then punishable by death) and discovered hitherto unknown parts of Africa, some of which belonged to native girls.

In other news ... Dame Annan Eagle was born today in 1904. I can't really tell you any more than that.

Oct 21

Truly great events spawn truly great quotations. Here are three from 21 October 1805, the day the British fleet under Horatio Nelson trounced the Franco-Spanish ships of Admiral Villeneuve at Trafalgar and saved England from invasion.

> *'England expects that every man shall do his duty.'*
> This was the coded message sent by a flag signalling system to the entire fleet by Nelson. He wanted to send 'England confides [trusts]' but they hadn't got that in the code book. It was the only cock-up the fleet made that day.

> *'Now, gentlemen, let us do something today which the world may talk of hereafter.'*
> Admiral Collingwood who led a column that smashed the enemy line (Nelson led the other).

> *'I do not say the French will not come; I only say they will not come by sea.'*
> Sorry, I can't remember whose this is, but it was a speech to the House of Commons, soon after Trafalgar (it was probably Lord Heseltine, nipping across from the Other Place).

In other news ... Katsushika Hokusai was born today in 1760.

Nobody, *nobody* does waves better (except Teasy-Weasey – and if you remember him, it's time for your cocoa).

Oct 22

'Pretty Boy' Floyd was killed today in 1934 in a gunfight with FBI agents. They were actually trying to find 'Gorgeous Features' Mulwinnie after a tip-off from 'Impossibly Handsome' Bomperini.

Isn't it funny how some famous people just aren't famous enough? In 1909, a woman flew an aircraft solo for the first time. That was quite an achievement, especially since women did not even have the vote in most European countries. Her name was Elise Deroche and it got me thinking about other 'greats' we've never heard of. There was: Eugene Sliced-Bread (of the Hertfordshire Sliced-Breads); the knight who invented champagne; the discoverer of the firelighter, Blaze Pascal; and Gertrude Stein, the beer mug manufacturer.

Where are they now?

Oct 23

Today marks the 370th anniversary of the battle Edge Hill in Warwickshire. It was the first battle of the English Civil War (I stress English here to remind our American cousins that we had one over two centuries before they did). The result was; Cavaliers 1, Roundheads 0. Did the Roundheads give up, realizing they were totally outclassed? No, they got God on their side and as for the Cavaliers it was all Down Hill after that.

In other news ... Leon Trotsky was expelled from the Communist Party today in 1926. He'd only heard about the bash on Facebook and turned up uninvited, insisting everybody needed the bottle of vodka he'd brought, not to mention the ice and the pick to go with it.

Uncle Joe Stalin didn't like Leon's status and is officially No Longer His Friend. So there!

Oct 24

Mrs Ann Taylor went over the Niagara Falls in a barrel today in 1901 to help pay the mortgage. Whoever thought it was a good idea to put up a Building Society at the foot of the Falls should have been certified. Incidentally, Mrs Taylor remained unhurt so at least she wasn't any broker.

In other news ... Today in 1861 the electric telegraph joined up across the States and that spelt the end for the Pony Express Company of Majors, Russell and Weddell. I think this was a shame. Just think how exciting it would be if, every time you sent an email or a message from your iPhone/iPad/Eyewash, a great hairy bloke in buckskins came galloping past and took it off you.

Oct 25

All right, this is the one you've all been waiting for. Balaclava Day, 1854. When 678 men of Lord Cardigan's Light Brigade (most of whom are sitting in 54mm replica in my attic) rode into the Valley of Death and into legend after a confused order took them the wrong way.

'It was a mad-brained trick, men,' Cardigan said to the survivors afterwards, 'but it was no fault of mine.'

'Go again, sir?' an anonymous soldier asked him. Makes you proud to be British, doesn't it?

In other news ... It was a good day for a battle today – Agincourt was fought in 1415 in the mud of Northern France. The French nobility were all but wiped out by a much smaller force, largely of archers, under Henry V. A while ago there was a move to have October 21 (Trafalgar Day) or October 25 (Agincourt Day) declared a public holiday in Britain, but that was shelved in case it upset our French colleagues in the EU. Actually, on the basis of that there ought to be no public holidays, because I can't think of a day when we didn't knock seven bells out of them.

Oct 26

Gilles de Rais was executed in Nantes today in 1440. Nobleman, Satanist, child molester and passing acquaintance of Joan of Arc, he was charged by the Catholic Church with Satanism and Heresy. Recently, a Catholic Court of Enquiry dismissed the charges against him. So, that just leaves the 140 or so children he is alleged to have murdered ...

In other news ... The Beatles got their MBEs today in 1965 much to the disgust of other MBE holders who sent theirs back. The inhabitants of a wildlife park in Chipping Sodbury also returned their Ancient Order of Buffalo medals.

Oct 27

Today in 1913, President Woodrow Wilson said, 'I want to take this occasion to say that the United States will never again seek one additional foot of territory by conquest.'
    Er ...

In other news ... Dylan Thomas, the Welsh poet, was born today in 1914. The midwife described him as a milk-sopping, bed-wetting sort of kid, Cartland-purple where he wasn't puce-pink, puking over the porcelain in the parlour while Captain Jack went out for a doubler and a pint.

Oct 28

Sir Richard Doll was born today in 1912. You probably haven't heard of him, but he is responsible for the greatest act of victimization of the twenty-first century. In establishing a link between lung cancer and smoking, he undoubtedly saved millions of lives, but he also caused the sad clusters of determined smokers, dying of frostbite and pneumonia outside pubs and nightclubs and for those mysterious, locked cabinets behind counters in supermarkets. You may have wondered why those poor, lost souls are sticking pins into a wax effigy – that is a likeness of Sir Richard, known as a Voodoo Doll.

In other news ... A Puritan college in Cambridge, Massachusetts got an injection of cash today from John Harvard who died of tuberculosis in 1638. The aim was that Harvard would one day rival Oxford or Cambridge.

Perhaps one day ...

Oct 29

An anonymous Belfast citizen got it absolutely right today in 1991 in the midst of appalling sectarian violence there -

> 'It's not the bullet with my name on it that worries me. It's the one that says, "To whom it may concern".'

In other news ... One of the great guys of Elizabethan England, Walter Ralegh, was executed today in 1618. The reason, those incomparable historians Sellar and Yeatman once said, was because he was left over from the previous reign. The real reason of course is that men as popular and larger than life as Ralegh had no place in the narrow world of that vicious paranoid freak, King James I.

Oct 30

Orson Welles frightened everybody today in 1938 when he produced and starred in a radio play based on H.G. Wells' *The War of the Worlds.* Even though the item was given plenty of publicity as fiction in advance, thousands of New Yorkers panicked and jammed roads and subways trying to leave the cities before the Martians arrived.

The knock-on effect was that when the British Prime Minister, Neville Chamberlain, announced that we were at war with Germany ten months later, everybody assumed it was a hoax and did nothing.

In other news ... The first television personality appeared on the screen today at the workshop of John Logie Baird in 1925. His name was William Taynton and the show was called *Britain's Got Taynton.* It was later serialised as a stupendously boring period piece called *Taynton Abbey.*

Oct 31

Jan Vermeer, the Dutch interior designer, was born today in 1632. He spent his entire artistic career painting kitchens, tiles and other rooms. One critic said his work was as 'dull as Dutchwater'. How true.

In other news ... 'Gentlemen,' said the Turkish leader Kemal Attaturk today in 1927, 'it was necessary to abolish the fez, which sat on the heads of our nation as an emblem of ignorance, negligence, fanaticism and hatred of progress ...' Which is pretty true, really. In the *great* days of the Ottoman Empire (fourteenth-seventeenth century) everybody wore turbans.

Mind you, the fez didn't do Tommy Cooper any harm.

November

Nov 1

L.S. Lowry was born today in 1887. He was one of those artists – Picasso, Klee, Mondrian, Klimt, Pollock and many, many more – who could draw and paint perfectly well, but just couldn't be arsed.

In other news ... 'A lie,' said Jim Callaghan, Britain's Prime Minister today in 1976, 'can be half way round the world before the truth has got its boots on.' That was 1976. Thanks to technology, Facebook, Twitter and Buboe, the speed of lying is *much* faster today.

Nov 2

Officially, the day of the dead in Catholic Mediterranean tradition – hmmm.
 Happy.

In other news ... Today in 1903, the *Daily Mirror* was launched, specifically as a newspaper for women. Great, I hear my good lady wife say, especially as that was the year the Women's Suffrage Union was set up. But wait, say I. The *Daily Mirror*'s readership had a reading age of 8, so there appears to be a teensy bit of condescension somewhere.
 Or is it just me?

Nov 3

Laika became the first dog in space today in 1957. She became the prototype for Pigs In Space if you're a Muppet fan. Come to think of it, she became the prototype for Pigs In Space if you're *not* a Muppet Fan. The Russians sent her into orbit on board Sputnik 2 and she reached Sirius (the Dog Star, get it?) last month. The Sputnik deniers of course don't believe a word of this.
 What *can* you do with people like that?

In other news ... Remember when American Presidents had

cool names, usually of a classical or Biblical bent? There was *Thomas* Jefferson, *Abraham* Lincoln, *Ulysses* Grant. What have we got today? Barack Obama. And tomorrow, if we're very unlucky? Mitten Romney!

And don't get me started on the Trump of Doom. Though hopefully, as I write, we are on track for another Biblical name – Joseph. 2025 Update: and so we were, but as things turned out, he was just Biden his time.

Nov 4

Native Americans were kicking ass today in 1791. Little Turtle, chief of the Miami tribe, beat the Americans under General Arthur St Clair. He'd already beaten General Harmer on the Wabash. Where was this guy in the 1890s?

In other news ... Anthony Eden said today in 1956, 'We are not at war with Egypt. We are in an armed conflict.' So that, children, is why a) we loused up the Suez crisis and b) why nobody remembers who Anthony Eden was.

Just a note to Eleven Bee Aitch – the above will not be accepted as reasons in your GCSE mocks coming up shortly. You have been warned.

Nov 5

All right, of course I'm bound to mention it. Today in 1605, the Gunpowder Plot was rumbled. Actually, it had been rumbled weeks before because the government, in the person of Robert Cecil, knew every move the plotters made. Just for the record, the original figure on the bonfire was not Guy Fawkes, but King James I. So if you're out cadging money from old ladies, you'll impress them more if you grab them by the lapels and snarl in their faces 'Penny for the James! Penny for the James!'

In other news ... My dear old uncle Robert, the Press Baron, mysteriously vanished today in 1991. He fell (or was he pushed?) off his yacht off the Canary Islands. We miss him deeply, of course, but it's not many Heads of Sixth Form at Comprehensive Schools who own a luxury yacht worth several million, so every cloud ...

Sadly, today finds me back at the chalk face after a nice half term break. With the nights dark and the mornings gloomy, I am just waiting now until the shortest day, when things begin to look up again. Chez Maxwell, Dec 21 is one of our favourite days, when the world starts spinning back towards spring. My mother-in-law, not a lady with a very merry disposition, prefers the longest day as everything from there is down hill to darkness and gloom. She doesn't even have a glass, never mind how full it might be.

Nov 6

I always felt a bit sorry for the Hawker Hurricane. It flew for the first time today in 1935, had 4 machine guns in each wing and a top speed of 325 mph at 20,000 feet. It was eclipsed by the Spitfire almost entirely because of the name. A Hurricane is a natural disaster; spitting fire is all about being unpleasant and deadly all in one.

In other news ... Adolphe Sax was born today in 1814 in Belgium (oh, what a shame!) and of course invented the Saxophone. It was not until the birth of John Philip Sousa, exactly forty years later, that anybody wrote music which involved the playing of one.

Nov 7

Benito Mussolini became leader of the National Fascist Party in Italy today in 1921. You've got to hand it to dictators – they have a great line in titles. Mussolini became Il Duce; Hitler was Der Fuhrer, Franco was El Caudillo. Even our own home-grown Oliver Cromwell was Lord Protector. And what have we got now? Minister for Sport, for the Environment, Levelling Up and Without Portfolio.

In other news ...

Helen Suzman, the anti-apartheid campaigner was born today in 1917. I just loved her in *Nicholas and Alexandra.*

Nov 8

Lord Lucan vanished today in 1974. He in all probability killed his children's nanny, Sandra
Rivett, in mistake for his wife and drove off into the night, leaving his car abandoned at Newhaven. Did he drown himself in the Channel? Hide out with Dr Josef Mengele in Paraguay? Become Banksy?

If you're reading this, my lord, time to come home, I think. You've 'lain doggo' for long enough.

In other news ... Edward Halley was born today in 1656. He was a Renaissance man years after the actual Renaissance and had a comet (Edward's Comet) named after him and went on to form an orchestra. He is the father of Halley Berry.

Nov 9

The Stealth bomber was unveiled today in 1988, a sneaky beast that can't be detected by radar, but can – as we now know – be shot down. I was idling my time during the First Gulf War in a London antique market and I heard a customer ask the stall owner if he had any bits of Stealth aircraft for sale. In those long-gone naïve days we all assumed he was a hopeful collector rather than a terrorist. Of course, the stall holder said, 'No, sorry, I'm afraid you're asking for the impossible.' He looked at the customer, winked and said, 'Come back tomorrow and I'll see what I can do.' I've often wondered whose side he was on.

In other news ... Charles de Gaulle died today in 1970. He was the one, according to *Allo! Allo!* with the big 'ooter. This man was leader of the Free French army during the Second World War and a complete pain in the backside to everybody he met. When they made the remake of *Day of the Jackal* I hoped the sniper would get him this time.

Nov 10

The Berlin Wall was smashed through in two places today in 1989, an iconic moment which effectively marked the beginning of the end of the 'evil empire' of the Communist Soviet Union. Pieces of the Wall became the new True Cross, relics which changed hands for large sums of money. There were so many pieces of the Wall on the market that there was clearly some confusion with the Wall of China. 'All in all,' as Pink Floyd once said, 'We're just another chink in the Wall.'

In other news ... Dick Jenkins was born today in 1925. Who he? I hear you cry. Well, he was a fine Shakespearean actor and famous drunk who married Liz Taylor sixteen times or thereabouts. Does that give you a clue?

Nov 11

At eleven o'clock this morning in 1918 the War to End Wars ended. The conflict that everybody said would be over by Christmas 1914 had lasted four years and 97 days. The stats are terrifying – 9 million dead, 27 million wounded. The Allies' bill was £68.5 billion; the Central Powers £32.6 billion.

And the world would never be the same again.

In other news ... I've never really understood Ned Kelly. He was an Australian outlaw hanged today in 1880 after a bank robbing career of just two years. He wore body armour – a breastplate and helmet made of iron. Perhaps he expected a role in *The Man in the Iron Mask*, then playing in the Melbourne Lyceum. Whatever the reason, the gear must have slowed him up a bit which probably enabled the Oz police to catch him in the first place.

Nov 12

John Bunyan, the Baptist preacher, was gaoled today in 1660 for preaching without a licence. In fact he spent years in gaol from time to time, clashing with the Quakers and the Church of

England. His son, Paul – a big lad – emigrated to the States and became a lumberjack where he clashed with Sequoias and Scots Pines.

In other news ... King Cnut died today in 1035. He was a brilliant ruler, warrior, statesman, law giver and all-round good egg. Yet people still spell his name Canute and trot out that stupid rubbish about the tide.

Nov 13

Mary Phelps Jacob did womankind a great service today in 1914 by patenting the 'backless brassiere', originally made out of two handkerchiefs and a piece of ribbon. The Germans used the far more expressive name *Bustenhalter* for the new gizmo which has caused generations of fumbling teenagers a great deal of trouble.

In other news ... An institution met for the first time today in 1920 which holds the record for the most feeble decisions in History. It met in Geneva and was called the League of Nations.

Nov 14

Today in 1952 the first 'Top Ten' of what the young people called the Hit Parade was published in NME (Not Musically Exciting). Vera Lynn was No 1 with 'Homing Waltz'. Jo Stafford was at No 2 with 'You Belong to my Heart' and Nat King Cole was third with 'Somewhere Along the Way'. All too soon, it was all going to get much, much worse.

In other news ... The worst bombing raid to hit Coventry was mounted tonight in 1940. The Cathedral was left a smoking shell, there were 554 deaths and 865 injured. 449 bombers dropped 503 tons of bombs. The phrase 'to coventrate' became part of the English language.

Nov 15

The Deutschmark was introduced in Weimar Germany today in 1923. Inflation was so galloping that a loaf of bread cost 200,000,000 marks. Anybody having a coffee in the Alexanderplatz in Berlin paid for it before they sat down. By the time they got up, it might cost ten times the starting price.

In other news ... William Pitt the Elder, the Earl of Chatham, was born today in 1708. Because of his relatively humble birth, he was sometimes called the Great Commoner. There were those who believed they didn't come any greater. And there were those who believed you couldn't be any commoner. Well done to his parents though, for their foresight in actually calling him William Pitt The Elder, Earl Of Chatham. A bit of a mouthful at the font, perhaps, but it no doubt helped him in his early parliamentary days.

Nov 16

A crowd of 200,000 watched today in 1724 as Jack Sheppard, safebreaker and highwayman was 'turned off' at Tyburn. Remember that odd little film *Where's Jack?* with Tommy Steele in the title role? Well, the real Jack was nearly that cute, apparently, with large, Johnny Depp style eyes and a slight stammer. He escaped *twice* from the condemned cell at Newgate and nobody knows quite how he did it. They just don't make rogues like him any more.

In other news ... 'It is beginning to be hinted that we are a nation of amateurs,' said Lord Rosebery today in 1900. The only annoying thing is that it took him so long to realize that.

Nov 17

Richard Nixon said today in 1973, 'I am not a crook' and that sent me in search of other serial deniers in History, e.g. –

- 'I am not, therefore I am' – Jean Paul Sartre
- 'I am not for turning' – Margaret Thatcher
- 'I am not going to invade Poland' – Adolf Hitler (1938)

- 'Oh, yes I am' – Adolf Hitler (1939)
- I am a knot garden' – Capability Brown

In other news ... The first successful British submarine voyage took place today in 1904 from Southampton to the Isle of Wight. The two principal ferry companies that serve the Island were both interested in acquiring the passenger franchise. But then they couldn't be arsed.

Further to this, Wightlink, or so my old mate M J Trow tells me, have axed umpteen sailings from their schedule, meaning that getting home after even the most modest evening out on the mainland is, for Islanders, darned near impossible. As a ferry is the only option they have, the uptake of theatre tickets and other treats will be markedly reduced and all the towns along the South Coast will see a knock-on effect as Islanders hunker down and watch paint dry at home instead of sallying forth to enjoy a night out. Well done, Wightlink, for trying to return a whole county to the Dark Ages. And come along, ferry entrepreneurs – you must be out there somewhere.

> **I wish I could say, eight years on, that things were now exponentially better.**
> **I wish ...**

Nov 18

In honour of National Doo Dah Day there is no blog for this Sunday.

We have been out to the Christmas shop, Heaven help us, and I have a strange time warp thing going on which is making History hard to fathom. Surely, Christmas 2011 was only last week? I know I keep finding bits of tinsel all over the house every time I move anything. So, either Christmas 2011 was last week, or Metternich is moonlighting as one of Santa's elves.

Nov 19

President Abraham Lincoln delivered one of the most brilliant speeches in History today in 1863. It was also one of the shortest and has come to be known as the Gettysburg Address. It's so brilliant it is worth quoting in full.

> 'Ladies and Gentlemen, my address is 339B John Wilkes Booth Road, Gettysburg.'

Absolutely brilliant.

In other news ... Today in 1908 a court in St Petersburg had to be adjourned because the prosecuting counsel refused to proceed against Russia's first female barrister. Tcha! I am forced to cry. They'll be demanding women bishops in the Church of England next ...

Wait a minute ...

Nov 20

Sir Anthony Blunt, Surveyor of the Queen's paintings, was stripped of his knighthood today in 1979 when it emerged that he was the 'fourth man' spying for the Russians along with Philby, Burgess and Maclean. And I was reminded of other notables whose titles had been removed over the years:

- Screaming Lord Sutch
- all of Lord Rockingham's Eleven
- Duke John Wayne
- Sirhan Sirhan
- **Barron Trump**

In other news ... Casimir Funk died today in 1967. Never heard of him? He was apparently the chappie who coined the word 'vitamin'. What a waste. With a fantastic name like his we could have had phrases like 'The disease is caused by a casimir deficiency' and 'Funk B12'. It's too late now.

Nov 21

Father Frances Xavier came back from two years in Japan today in 1551. He was the first Westerner to live among the Japanese and said of them '... no finer people will be found.'

That's because he wasn't building the Burma-Thailand Railway.

In other news ... Today in 1906 a man died in Glasgow when 300,000 gallons of whisky burst out of vats. He had to get out three times to go to the loo.

What do you mean, you've heard it before? It was pretty new in 1906.

Nov 22

We all remember where we were today in 1963. There was a nightmare on Elm Street, Dallas as somebody gunned down John F Kennedy, riding through the city in an open-topped Lincoln convertible with his wife, Jackie and the governor of Texas, John Connolly and his wife. Millions of words, umpteen documentaries, a handful of movies, official and unofficial enquiries and nearly half a century – and still we don't know who did it.

In other news ... Richard Strauss unveiled his new opera today in Dresden. The year was 1901 and the opera was about a team of dedicated scientists beavering away to cure the common cold. It was called Feuersnot.

Nov 23

You know my views on Crippen. Even before we realized that the body in the basement of his house at 63 Hilldrop Crescent couldn't have been Mrs Crippen (Belle Elmore) because it was male, I thought they should have given him a medal because she was so horrible. Everybody disagreed of course and they hanged him at Pentonville today in 1910.

The Tufnell Park One is innocent.

In other news ... Bill Pratt was born today in 1887. Who he, I hear you ask. He became Boris Karloff in later life, legend of

Frankenstein, The Mummy and *The Body Snatcher*. Other film stars who weren't going to make it with their own monikers include:

- Laruska Skikne (Laurence Harvey)
- Issur Danielovitch (Kirk Douglas)
- Diana Fluck (Diana Dors)
- Frances Gumm (Judy Garland) 〇
- George Crane (Randolph Scott)
- Bacteria Cuniculus (Bugs Bunny).

Nov 24

The deeply unpleasant misogynist, John Knox, died today in 1572. Scottish Protestants think he was the best thing since sliced bread but then there were those who thought Adolf Hitler was a pretty good egg too.

In other news ... Charles Darwin published his *Origin of Species* today in 1859. Two things to note about this –

1. Of three famous books published in the same year (Darwin's, Samuel Smiles's *Self Help* and Mrs Beeton's *Household Management*) only Mrs Beeton went on to make any money.
2. Some people today still regard Darwin's natural selection as a theory only. Didn't they watch *Inherit the Wind?*

Nov 25

Yesterday I mentioned Charles Darwin. He was never quite able to include Man in his natural selection argument, but others did, especially Thomas Huxley who wiped the floor spectacularly with Bishop 'Soapy Sam' Wilberforce of the Church of England in Oxford in 1860. The question of the authority of the Bible was much talked about and today in 1864, the Conservative Party's 'hatchet man', Benjamin Disraeli, famously said, 'Is man an ape or an angel? I, my lord, am on the side of the angels.'

Except that William Gladstone, the Liberal Party and an awful lot of Conservatives, disagreed with that.

In other news ... The KKK got back together again today in 1915 in Georgia. The original Klan targeted the newly-freed slaves after the Civil War but this one targeted:

- Blacks
- Jews
- Catholics
- Immigrants
- Communists
- Pacifists
- Darwinians.

The Klan is in decline today because there is almost nobody who is considered fit to join.

Nov 26

New York had its first streetcar (horse drawn of course) today in 1832. It ran between 14th and Spring Street and was called Desire.

Of course.

In other news ... One of the most spectacular finds in archaeology took place today in 1922 when Howard Carter and his backer, the Earl of Caernarvon, broke through to the uninvaded tomb chambers of the Egyptian pharaoh Tutankhamen in the Valley of the Kings.

Just think – without that we would never have had the Indiana Jones series ...

Nov 27

Women Policemen appeared on Britain's streets today in 1914 (I have been obliged to insert this piece on account of my good lady wife – Inspector Carpenter-Maxwell – having me in a half

Nelson). The uniform was awful and it had three little buttons at the side of the mid-calf length skirt so that they could unbutton them to chase baddies. What could they do once they caught them? Nothing. This was only an experiment and they weren't given powers of arrest until 1922. Presumably they had to ask Chummy to stay put while they went in search of a real policeperson. Ouch – the Mem's half Nelson has now turned into a Full Nelson and I've lost the use of one arm and am blind in one eye.

In other news ... A Bible printed in the fifteenth century was sold at Christie's auction house today in 1991. The Good Book? It had better be – it cost £1.1 million!

Nov 28

The German physicist Max [no relation] Planck said it all today in 1934 when he wrote, 'A new scientific truth does not triumph by convincing its opponents and making them see the light but rather because its opponents eventually die out and a new generation grows up that is familiar with it.'

So, in reality, every word of the Bible is true; the earth is about 6,000 years old (and flat); Phlogiston occurs in every chemical experiment; Frank Sinatra had a good singing voice and babies are delivered by storks.

I knew it!

In other news ... Horse racing was banned today in 1967 because of an epidemic of Foot and Mouth disease. Whenever such disasters occur, the government of the day leaps in with ludicrous, over-the-top measures. Foot and Mouth? Destroy all cattle. Salmonella in eggs? Destroy all chickens. Oil tanker spillages? Destroy all tankers. Global warming? Stop spraying your armpits.

Actually, nature has been coping with all these issues for centuries, without the help of the British government or its biased, obsessive scientific think tanks.

And on a personal level, it would be not humanly possible to be in a room with up to twenty teenage boys without the addition of many gallons of Lynx. You may mock that most sledgehammer of deodorants, but without it ... I don't want you to even have to imagine it!

Nov 29

Today was the day, in 1831, when the Duke of Wellington famously described his soldiers as 'the scum of the earth, enlisted for drink'. He went on to say (and this is hardly ever added to the quotation) 'but we have made men of them.'

Good old Nosey!

In other news ... The first English newspaper went on sale today in 1641. It offered a dream fortified manor house; you could send for a CD of Thomas Tallis's Greatest Hits and the Sports Pages were full of the latest Real Tennis scandals in which the game's audience shouted racist insults at the players.

The start of a great tradition.

P.S. Sir Peregrine Leveson agreed and said he saw a great future for the Press and what a fine job King Charles was doing running the country.

Nov 30

An era came to an end today in 1936 when Joseph Paxton's Crystal Palace burnt down. Built in 1851 for the Great Exhibition, the astonishing building, of glass and wrought iron, was moved to Sydenham Park where it continued to be an attraction. The flames could be seen as far away as Brighton and even to the last, the Palace drew crowds – special trains were laid on to watch it burn.

They had a chance to rebuild the Palace in 2000 for the Millennium but did they? Oh, no. They built the O2 instead ....

In other news ... Oscar Wilde died today in 1900 in Paris. Dazzling wit, playwright, raconteur, he fell foul of the bigotry of Britain (especially the rabid anti-homosexuality Act of Henry

Labouchere MP) and died in poverty. He is buried in the great cemetery of Pere Lachaise. Pay your respects next time you're there.

DECEMBER

Dec 1

If you're a fan, like me, of Sellar and Yeatman's masterly *1066 And All That,* you'll know that Henry I of England died of a surfeit of lampreys. A what? I hear you cry, dear reader. Well, a lamprey is an eel and a surfeit is too many. All this happened today in 1135 which is long before they had sell-by dates etc. I can't help thinking that as the bloke was 66 (which was *ancient* in the twelfth century) it was probably time he shuffled off this mortal coil anyway.

What did he leave behind? A squabble between potential rulers Matilda and Stephen and a series of excellent novels by Ellis Peters.

In other news ... The Cross Channel diggers met in the middle today in 1990, nearly completing a multi-million pound project linking Britain to France. There was a great deal more earth movement when everybody from Harold Godwinson (d 1066) on turned in their graves.

Dec 2

'As I write,' said Henry Longfellow today in 1859, 'they are leading old John Brown to execution ... This is sowing the wind to reap the whirlwind, which will soon come.'

It did. Instead of realizing that (however loony) Brown was right and setting free the slaves there and then, the Civil War broke out leading to more American deaths than in all other wars put together.

In other news ... Hernan Cortes, the Spanish conquistador, died today in 1547. Thousands of Incas cheered. He died from drinking, according to a poem, too much stout, although his pet Peke may have been involved. For those who don't know about the famous conqueror, he stood upon his Peke in Darien, and probably, though it is unrecorded, got a nasty bite, which went septic.

Or something like that.

Dec 3

Dom Gregory Dix, a British monk, said today in 1977, 'It is no accident that the symbol of a bishop is a crook and the sign of an archbishop is a double cross.'

Whose side was this guy on?

In other news ... Agatha Christie vanished today in 1925 and was missing for several days. Sadly, they found her again.

Dec 4

Nicholas Breakspear became the only Englishman to be elected to the Papacy today in 1154. After that, it was mostly Italians, with a few Frenchmen. And for all you feminists out there, 'Pope Joan' was only fictional – soz.

In other news ... President Rutherford B Hayes told Congress today in 1877 -

> 'Many, if not most, of our Indian wars have had their origins in broken promises and injustice on our part.'

He got that absolutely right, but most of white America wasn't listening and the massacre at Wounded Knee was still to come.

Dec 5

One of the coolest sentences was passed today in 1991 by Judge Edwin Torres in the United States. He said, 'Your parole officer has not yet been born.'

In other news ... The Bermuda Triangle nonsense began today in 1945 when five planes out of Fort Lauderdale in Florida vanished somewhere beyond the Keys. The flight leader reported that they were lost, their instruments were going haywire and 'even the sea looks different'. A rescue plane sent up to find them disappeared too, paving the way for Atlantis theories, black holes, white dwarfs and Erich von Daniken et al.

No amount of sensible theories – such as typhoons, hurricanes, contrary winds, engine/radio defects or plain old pilot error – will ever replace this. It will vanish and vanish.

Dec 6

'The Soviet Union has disintegrated,' said Leonid Kravachuk of the Ukraine today in 1991. This was far too late for thousands of innocent people who went to their deaths under Lenin, Trotsky and above all, Stalin in the name of a political system that cannot possibly work in a free society.

In other news ... The French tennis team won the Davis Cup today in 1991 and their captain, Yannick Noah, spoke for them all when he said, 'Guy was happy, I was happy, the team was happy, the crowd was happy, everybody was happy. There is just one word to describe it all – happiness.'

Had a way with words, didn't he, old Yannick?

Dec 7

'A date which will live on in infamy' as F.D. Roosevelt called this day in 1941. Without warning, the Japanese Pacific fleet attacked the American naval base at Pearl Harbor in Hawaii. There was no formal declaration of war before 200 aircraft were destroyed and 2,400 men killed. The whole story was brilliantly told in the film *Tora! Tora! Tora!* and crappily told in *Pearl Harbor.*

In other news ... Marshal Michel Ney, 'the bravest of the brave' was executed by firing squad today in 1815. He had been sent to arrest Napoleon who had escaped from Elba and was back on French soil. He promised to bring 'la bête noire' back to Paris in a cage. In the event, he re-joined his old master and told the newly-restored Bourbon dynasty (they of biscuits) where to stick it. Miffed, they had him shot.

Dec 8

Sammy David Jnr was born today in 1925. Billing himself as a 'one-eyed Jewish black man', his stand-up was legendary. He used 25 pounds of Brylcreem on his hair every day and was the fastest man with a six-shooter never to appear in a Western.

In other news ... Thomas de Quincey died today in 1859. He suffered from facial neuralgia, gave up school and Oxford University, lived as a beggar in London, was constantly broke and smoked opium. Despite all this he lived to be seventy-four. What an advert for declassifying drugs!

Dec 9

Who said, 'I am like an unpopular electric eel in a pond full of flatfish'? Was it:-

   a) Clarence Birdseye, the pioneer of frozen food?
   b) Rick Stein, piscatorial chef?
   c) Somebody out of *Finding Nemo*?
   d) Edith Sitwell?

I entered the above to show my displeasure at multi-choice answers in school examinations. Were these invented by:

   a) Arnold Toynbee, Emeritus Professor of Oxford University?
   b) Jeremy Paxman, boring old fart who worked on University Challenge?
   c) Chris Tarrant?
   d) The Coughing Major?

In other news ... Aneurin Bevan, founder of the NHS and Labour MP, said, on this day in 1953, 'We know what happens to people who stay in the middle of the road. They get run over.'

He was talking, of course, of the Liberal Democrat party of the future.

And it was wishful thinking.

Dec 10

It may surprise you – it certainly surprised me – to discover that the first territory in America to give women the vote was Wyoming, 143 years ago today. Then I realized that there were 428,000 men in Wyoming in 1869, 3.2 million cattle and two women.

Heigh ho.

In other news .... Alfred Nobel won the world's prize for biggest idiot today in 1892 when he said that his dynamite invention would put an end to war. On the contrary, it increased battlefield casualties a hundredfold.

Nice one, Alfred – back to the drawing board, old son!

Dec 11

Herbert Asquith, the politician, said today in 1920 – 'Things are being done in Ireland which would disgrace the blackest annals of the lowest despotism in Europe.'

That's a bit of a harsh description of the setting up of Boyzone, if you ask me.

In other news ... Charlie Chaplin's bowler and cane were sold today in 1987 at Christie's auction house for £82,500. His boots went for £38,500. Sadly, his underpants failed to reach their reserve.

Dec 12

'I called the New World into existence to redress the balance of the Old,' said George Canning, the British Foreign Minister today in 1826. He was referring to the fact that Britain had given cash, recognition and above all the guns of the Royal Navy to the new South American republics trying to break away from Portugal and Spain.

And how did they repay us? They hid escaping Nazis after 1945 and invaded the Falklands in 1982.

Thanks, guys.

In other news ... In New York today in 1907, a statute was passed insisting that girls about to be married should sign affidavits declaring their age and good conduct. This is clearly a good idea. My good lady wife has just read this blog over my shoulder and

Dec 13
Leighford General Hospital.

No, no. It's nothing, really. They say I'll be out by Christmas.

Jacob Fussell made history today in Baltimore in 1903 when he invented a cone for eating ice cream. No spoon was required and there was no mess. But somewhere along the line it all went pear shaped. I can remember in the 1980s we were all given a special phone number to report the number of cones on Motorways.
    Where did it all go wrong?

In other news ... Lord Alfred Douglas, known as 'Bosie', the friend of Oscar Wilde, was sentenced to six months in gaol today in 1923 for libelling Winston Churchill. Now, I loathe Alfred Douglas and I loathe Winston Churchill, so it's a bit of a win/win situation for me.

Dec 14

Roald Amundsen, the Norwegian explorer, reached the South Pole today in 1911, the first man to do so. He left the Norwegian flag there and a note for Robert Falcon Scott leading a British team trying to beat him there. It simply said 'Bobby – Nah-Nah-di-Nah-Nah. Love, Ro.'

In other news ... Max [no relation] Planck came out with the quantum leap notion in Physics today in 1900. Not everybody was impressed. Isaac Newton turned in his grave and Alfred Nobel coined the expression 'thick as a Planck'.

Dec 15

Two great Americans died today, seventy-six years apart. The first was Sitting Bull, spiritual leader of the Lakota whose victory over Custer's 7th Cavalry has passed into legend. He spent some years in prison and travelled with Bill Cody's Wild West Show, spoofing the Indian Wars. By the year of his death (1890) however he had joined the Ghost Shirt movement dedicated to the restoration of the Plains Indians' way of life. He was shot and killed in a skirmish with troops sent to suppress the cult.

The other was Walt Disney.

In other news ... The body of Napoleon Bonaparte was reburied in Les Invalides in Paris today in 1840. He had died in 1821 on St Helena, poisoned either by the British or the wallpaper, whichever version you choose to believe, and it took nearly twenty years for the body to be transferred.

You would think the French could have built a more fitting tomb for their greatest son (yes, I know, he wasn't exactly French, but you can't have everything). The tomb is a huge, ugly slab of marble – yeuch!

Dec 16

Anna Steenkamp, a Boer farmer's wife, wrote in her diary today in 1836 – 'It was not the nonwhites' freedom that drove us to such lengths [travelling north in the Great Trek] as their being placed on an equal footing with Christians, contrary to the laws of God.'

You can't get a more Christian sentiment than that, now, can you?

In other news ... The world went mad today in 1991, when the name of the new leader of MI5 – 'M' – was printed in the British Press. She was Stella Rimmington, the first woman to hold the job. This marked the end of the spying game as far as Britain was concerned – not that a woman was in charge (he added hastily) but that the whole thing was so public. This explains why James Bond had to undergo so many plastic surgery operations. The name was the same, but in a feeble attempt to pretend the

Secret Services were still secret, the face had to change.

Spooky.

Dec 17

Orville Wright said today in 1903 (after making four flights of less than a minute each at Kitty Hawk Beach, Carolina) 'The airplane stays up because it doesn't have the time to fall.'

Er ... needs work, Orv.

In other news ... Sir Humphrey Davy was born today in 1778. He wasn't Sir Humphrey then, of course; that accolade came later, after he'd invented the safety lamp for miners and discovered sodium, calcium, barium, potassium, magnesium and strontium by passing electricity through molten metal compounds.

Nobody likes a smartarse, Humphrey!

Dec 18

When David, Prince of Wales (he who later became a Nazi and married a bloke called Mrs Simpson if you believe various theories) asked the Commander in Chief of the army, Lord Kitchener, if he could go to the Front in the First World War (this was 1914, by the way) the Field Marshal replied, 'I don't mind your being killed but I object to your being taken prisoner'.

Thanks, Kitch. Right back atchya!

In other news ... Joseph Grimaldi was born today in 1779. When he developed the white face clown make-up, he thought he was adding to the laughs and lustre of the circus. Unfortunately, he was only prefiguring all those creepy killer-clown movies of the Seventies onwards and condemning generations of people to a life lived under the weight of their coulrophobia.

Incidentally, Mrs B., cleaner of this parish, is a renowned coulrophobe. She once knocked Mr B unconscious because he jumped out at her suddenly wearing a glace cherry on his nose and precious little else. Or at least, that's her story and she's sticking to it.

Dec 19

It was a bad day for Russia today in 1991 when Mikhail Gorbachev resigned. The architect of *perestroika* and *glasnost*, he handled the collapse of the USSR with flair and skill. He was replaced by a drunk, Boris Yeltsin.

In other news ... Ralph Richardson was born today in 1902. One of the best-known classical actors of his generation, he excelled in Shakespearean roles but also took to films like a duck to water. I stand to be corrected, but I think he was the only actor to play William Gladstone in the history of the cinema. He could also be seen roaring around the Home Counties on a powerful motorbike when in his seventies. To our minds (the collective known as the Carpenter-Maxwells, that is) his best cinema moment was as the Supreme Being in *Time Bandits*. But that's us for you.

The Trows concur. Best line: 'Well, I *am* the nice one.'

Dec 20

The Gallipoli campaign ended in disaster today in 1915. The idea was to hit 'the soft underbelly of Europe' by attacking the Turks via Constantinople (that's Istanbul to you, Eleven Eff Eight) but it all went horribly pear-shaped. First the Royal Navy chickened out believing there were hundreds of mines across the Straits called the Dardanelles (there were only four left when they came to this decision). So the army had to go in alone and landed from rowing boats while being machine-gunned from the dunes. The Turks were stiffened by crack German troops and the Allies never had enough men, guns or ammunition (especially high explosives) because these things were needed at the Western Front in France.

Ironically the best thing about Gallipoli was the withdrawal, accomplished in one night, in total secrecy. The enemy had no idea we'd gone. Those responsible? Winston Churchill – ridiculous, ambitious ideas, ill thought-out; Lord Kitchener – too mean with the hardware; General Sir Ian Hamilton, local commander – no clue.

In other news ... Boris Yeltsin (see yesterday's blog) announced today in 1991 that Russia wanted to join NATO. He also wanted flying pigs, three pink elephants and life membership of the Bullingdon Club.

Dec 21

This was the day in 1978 when Denis Healey famously described Geoffrey Howe's attack on his budget proposals as 'like being savaged by a dead sheep'.

Howe had the last laugh, however. When he was made a member of the House of Lords, his crest was a vicious-looking wolf in sheep's clothing.

Nice one.

In other news ... Walt Disney's *Snow White and the Seven Dwarves* appeared on American cinema screens today in 1935 ushering in a brilliant new era of cartooning. Today's techniques have eclipsed it but it's still a marvellous film and the old crone with her poisonous apple is still every child's nightmare, even today.

The porn version – *Snow White and the Seven Perverts* – failed to make much of an impact.

And, of course, the End of the World is no longer nigh – again. I was out shopping in Leighford High Street this morning at 11.11 and it was eerie .... everything went on exactly as normal. So, all you girls of Ten Pea Zed, come out from under your duvets and stop sobbing and texting each other – it was *only a story*. Perhaps you'll listen to me next time ... now that *would* be the end of the world!

I suppose I should write tomorrow's blog, now we are still here!

Dec 22

James Edward Stuart, son of the deposed James II, landed at Peterhead in Scotland today in 1715. Rightfully king of England, his aim was to overthrow the usurper, George I, who was the son of the usurper Electress Sophie, who was a cousin of the usurper Anne, who was the sister and sister-in-law respectively of Mary and William who had taken the throne from James's dad in the first place. (Do keep up, Seven Bee Four; it really couldn't be simpler).

So, despite a promising start, why did James not succeed in getting his throne back? He was only Pretending.

In other news ... Mary Ann Evans died today in 1880. She is better known as George Eliot and used the male nom de plume to get her novels published in a male-dominated, sexist world. That got me thinking of other writers whose real names should be exposed e.g. Ellis Peters (Edith Pargeter); Currer Bell (Charlotte Bronte) and Andy McNab (Priscilla-May Blenkinsop).

Dec 23

Joseph Hansom patented his famous 'safety cab' today in 1834. Not only did he create the best-known image of the nineteenth century street scene, but he paved the way for that immortal line in Kenneth Horne's *Beyond Our Ken* on the radio (circa 1964) – 'My name is immaterial. Sir James Immaterial. And I am talking of a time when England was full of Hansom cabs and ugly furniture.'

They don't write them like that any more.

In other news ... Vincent van Gogh cut off his earlobe today. The usual explanation for this is that
1. he was mad
2. he'd had a row with Paul Gaugin.

In fact, it all happened because he saw Gaugin's work and said, 'Paul, me ol' mucker, I'd give my right ear to be able to paint as good as like what you do.'

And of course, he was mad.

Dec 24

'Twas the night before Christmas and in 1828 William Burke went on trial in Edinburgh for the murder of Daft Jamie and grave robbery. Note to the legal profession and every other organization (except teaching, of course) that closes for two-three weeks around Christmas time – IN OLDEN TIMES PEOPLE ACTUALLY WORKED FOR A LIVING!

In case you're interested, Burke and his accomplice Hare (who got off by stitching up his mate) were robbing graves and murdering people to sell the bodies to anatomists who needed freshish corpses for dissection. Burke was found guilty and hanged and – how neat is this? – dissected.

In other news ... They thought they'd found Lord Lucan today in 1974. He was the chappie, you'll remember, who did a runner after allegedly murdering his children's nanny. In fact, 'Lucan' turned out to be John Stonehouse, a rather dodgy MP who was believed to have drowned off Miami but had in fact faked his own death.

You really couldn't make it up!

Dec 25

All right, let's get this over with. Christians will tell you that Jesus is the reason for the season (i.e. the celebration of the birth of Christ on this day 2012 years ago). Actually, of course, they are almost certainly wrong. Until the 5th century, some people celebrated the man's birthday in January, others in May, others with the Feast of the Epiphany. In 440 a synod of the Church pinched the old Roman midwinter festival (already an excuse for a holiday) and claimed it was 25 December. There is no historical justification for this and so those who bemoan the fact that the whole nativity thing is disappearing from Christmas and we all just use it as an excuse to eat and drink too much and watch excruciatingly awful TV, is not surprising, really.

In other news ... The Florentine monk Giralomo Savonarola got a bit shirty today in 1497. While everybody else was watching the Queen's Speech or yet another chance to see all 438 ghastly episodes of Downton on the tele, he accused the Pope of corruption and Leonardo da Vinci of sodomy.

Come off the fence, now, Savvy and tell it like it is.

Despite this somewhat unseasonal post, I would nevertheless like to wish my follower the very warmest compliments of the season. Nolan, Metternich and Mrs Carpenter-Maxwell all join me in hoping you are having a splendid Christmas, with as many presents as you wanted and more turkey than you could possibly eat in a long day's march. Taking a leaf out of my old mate M.J. Trow's family book, we have bought Nolan his first guitar, which is sounding not too bad at all from the sitting room. By all accounts if he takes to it, it will lead to a life of penury for us as more and more sophisticated instruments become necessary, but if music helps him grow up into half the man Tali Trow has, then it will be money well spent.

God Bless Us, Every One!*

* *Tiptoe Through the Tulips* ©Tiny Tim Music 1971

Dec 26

The Feast of Stephen. One of the greatest artists of all time died today in 1909. He was Frederic Remington and he specialized in scenes of the Wild West. His horses, cattle, cowboys and Indians are simply superb, *and* he could sculpt his designs with equal skill. What a talent! Unfortunately, he was only forty when he died – a great loss to the world of art.

In other news ... American film star Richard Widmark was born today in 1914. I never saw him put in a bad performance and he was notoriously fast on the draw. Legend has it that that was why he had a damaged hand in *Warlock*, so that Henry Fonda could outdraw him.

Fed up with the turkey yet? I am looking forward to supper tonight with M.J. Trow and family. Yum.

Dec 27

Three greats of the cinema were born today but not in the same year. Sydney Greenstreet (1879) was a marvellous heavy (literally!) in noir films like *The Maltese Falcon*. Marlene Dietrich (1901) was a fine-boned German actress who smouldered magnificently in *The Blue Angel* and *Destry Rides Again*. And then there was Gerard Depardieu ...

In other news ... The world was changed forever today in 1831 when HMS *Beagle* set sail from Devonport on a five year scientific expedition. On board was young Charles Darwin who would take one look at the wrinkly old critters on the Galapagos Islands and know at once that the Old Testament was just a story about Jewish folk. He immediately went into print (twenty-eight years later) with his book *Origin of Species*.

Dec 28

On this day in 1904 the first weather reports were published in London by wireless telegraphy. This was a great opportunity for the Meteorological Office to get it totally wrong using a different medium, something they still excel at today.

In other news ... *TW3 (That Was The Week That Was)* was closed down today in 1963 because it was an election year (no Big Brother pressure there then). Like its successor, *Spitting Image*, it caricatured politicians and celebrities and introduced naughty themes on our television sets. We have nothing like this now, except a procession of tawdry, foul-mouthed blokes who are referred to (for only partially obvious reasons) as stand-up comedians.

Dec 29

Today in 1170, four knights led by Reginald FitzUrse (the name means, literally, bastard bear) crashed into the cathedral at Canterbury and sliced off the top of the head of the Archbishop, Thomas Becket. They almost certainly operated on the orders of the king, Henry II, who was rather miffed that his old friend Thomas had gone all religious on him (even though he'd given him the Archbishop's gig in the first place).

It is a reflection on the times, perhaps, that today, saying that Rowan Williams and Justin Welby weren't very good as the A of C is about as vicious as it gets.

In other news ... William Gladstone was born today in 1809. Despite spending most of his life in England, he retained an irritating Lowland Scots accent to the end (much to the annoyance of Queen Victoria, he didn't die until 1898). We actually have him taped (they all did!) on phonograph.

Dec 30

Rasputin was murdered today in 1916 by Prince Felix Yusopov at the nobleman's house in St Petersburg. The house is still there. 'Rasputin' means the debauched one (**so presumably, Vladimir is the bauched one**) and he certainly enjoyed the company of titled ladies (even, it was rumoured, the Tsarina), drank like a fish and exposed himself in various restaurants. The stories of his death were much exaggerated. Allegedly, he was poisoned (in his wine and cakes), shot, bashed with chains, tied up and thrown into the frozen river Neva. When they pulled him out two days later, it was said that he still had had the strength to snap the rope.

Wow.

In other news ... Anita Loos got it right today in the *Observer* in 1973 when she wrote 'I'm furious about the Women's Liberationists. They keep ... proclaiming that women are brighter than men. That's true, but it should be kept very quiet or it ruins the whole racket.'

Dec 31

Well, that's it – the Year of Blogging Dangerously is over. So it just remains for me to say thank you for your company in 2012 and in 2013 may you have all the good things you could wish for – with love from the Maxwell-Carpenters and all at Leighford High. Perhaps we will meet again in the New Year – you'll know me when you see me, I'm sure.

> And it's good night from me, as well. I read and loved this blog when it was brand new in 2012 and am delighted to have been given the chance to check it over for typos (none, obv) and make some up to date additions where needed. Thank you, Max for your company for more years than I care to remember and for being the teacher I always wanted to be.